POSITIVE POWER

12 STEPS TO MASTERING YOUR MINDSET

SARAH HALL

This book is dedicated to you; for your conscious decision to maintain a better way of life. This book is for those who don't believe in mediocrity, for those who want to ignite their lives and cast magical spells that transform their dreams into their realities... this book is for you to really start living.

With love, Sarah Hall

CONTENTS

2020 EDITION

Welcome to Positive Power – 12 Steps to Mastering your Mindset!

I am thrilled to have you here, and if this is the first time that you are discovering this book then I am so excited for the journey you are about to go on. Your life is about to change.

Since this is the revised edition of the book in 2020, you should know that in the past few years many more transformations have happened in my own life through the application of these steps, and there are so many more incredible things on their way as well!

I traveled around the world for 5 months on a solo journey staying at some of the most beautiful places in the world, including Monaco, all across France, Italy, Belgium, several Greek islands, St. Tropez, Sardinia, and so many other stunning locations which you can see on my YouTube channel, Wealthy Optimist.

I went to Cambodia on a peace mission for 3 weeks and volunteered helping impoverished communities and women who escaped the sex trafficking industry in 7 provinces across the country. This trip changed my life and my outlook on how I can truly give back to others.

I became a stunt performer in TV and Film, performing stunts on huge TV shows like 'Lost in Space', which is currently on Netflix. This was something I always dreamed of and it absolutely lived up to my expectations of how much fun it would be!

I moved across the world from Vancouver, Canada to London, UK by myself – knowing absolutely no one in London – and I now have a beautiful apartment here. I go for runs along the river every day in a gorgeous part of London that is highly sought after. I'm getting my citizenship for the UK, something I used to dream about doing which is now happening right before my eyes.

I am blessed to be able to travel whenever I want. The world is at my fingertips and I have created the freedom to explore it.

I have positive people in my life, having released and removed any negative friends, created healthy boundaries with family and taken back my power from the person who sexually abused me, a traumatic experience that nearly ruined my life and destroyed my self-confidence for over a decade.

I have freed myself from abusive, toxic relationships and created healthy boundaries for myself which has enabled me to draw in the right people who want the best for me. I am now able to create a healthy, safe relationship where we support one another and use communication consistently to grow a loving, balanced and respectful bond.

I have developed and constantly practice coping skills for my anxiety and C-PTSD that I developed from years of trauma, sexual abuse, physically and emotionally abusive relationships and grief from the loss of my older sister and other people close to me.

I have overcome addiction through the application and practice of the steps in this book and the support of incredibly strong, supportive people in my life. I realized that I can support others when they don't have a support system, and I now coach people who need help through their emotional battles and to build a life full of love, self-respect and joy.

We are continuously growing our amazing community both online and around the world, inspiring others and helping them through my coaching program and in our online communities which include:

- Our 'Wealthy Optimist Coaching' group on Facebook
- My Facebook Page; Wealthy Optimist
- My YouTube Channel; Wealthy Optimist
- My Podcast; Wealthy Optimist
- My Instagram; @SarahHallAuthor

I've truly created a life of freedom, abundance and joy through the steps within this book, and I am sharing them with you so that you can transform your own life and start living a life that you used to only dream of. You need to know from this moment on that anything is possible.

INTRODUCTION

Life is for the living.

This is a saying that bears a world of truth. Life is not for those who wake up without any real purpose.

Life, as it was meant to be, is to be enjoyed in abundance and without stress. Of course, every obstacle we face is supposed to make us stronger. But the mere belief in the foregoing statement is what validates it.

How are we to live, enjoy life, and overcome challenges and obstacles, if not positively?

Positive living is more than just two words that have become a trend for motivational speakers and life coaches. It is sung so casually that while we have all heard it, very few of us actually understand what it means to truly be positive. Being positive is a reality; it is what we all need in order to excel in life. It is not a cliché; it is a fact. It is not redundant; it should be re-emphasized.

For you who have chosen to read this book: it is no coincidence. There is something you can learn here. You may find it on the first page, you may it find in the middle, or at the end of the book. Or you may, like so many others, take knowledge from each chapter, growing more and more with each day as an individual in your new positive way of thinking.

The next chapters are dedicated to you. You, who would do more with the time they have here on earth. Who would make every second count. Who would explore the depths of their existence by following their passions with enthusiasm and courage. For you, these chapters will guide you on your path.

Most importantly, this book is dedicated to those who would find strength in overcoming obstacles and challenges. To those who are looking for the positive side of life. For those who have always felt a stir inside their souls... A whisper of greatness but weren't sure how to set it free.

This book is for you to learn how to unleash your inner magic once and for all!

Here's to you.

WHAT IS POSITIVITY?

Have you ever seen a number line? In mathematics, a number line is defined as a straight, horizontal line with numbers placed at even points along its the length of the line. It's not a ruler, so the spacing between each number isn't relevant, and the numbers can be extended indefinitely, but for the purpose of this example we will extend it to 10 on each side.

Here, I'll break it down for everyone who has math skills like mine—not the best.

In the center of the number line we have zero. We can also call that the neutral zone. Everything to the left of the Number 0 is negative and everything to the right is positive.

This is simple mathematics. In fact, if you think back far enough, you'll probably remember learning it in school at a young age.

You might be thinking, 'why is the number line important to mindset and personal development?' Well, let me tell you a little story about myself to shed some light on it.

When I was a child there were no shades of gray. There was only black and white. Things either were to my liking, or they were not. I either got the ice cream I asked for (ever so politely I might add), or I was completely shut down (devastating, I know).

That was until an experience changed me. I was turning seven and had I spent weeks mentally preparing myself for this special day. Anyone who knows me knows just how much I love my birthday. It's my favourite holiday—don't even try to tell me it shouldn't be celebrated as such! I even go as far as scheduling the day off from work, a tradition that I've upheld ever since my first job. But this birthday... well, I remember this birthday like it was yesterday.

I woke up early to a bright and sunny morning. It was one of those magical childhood birthdays that fall on a weekend, so all my friends were invited to my party and none of us had to go to school the next day. I remember thinking it was going to be the best day ever.

I went to breakfast in my party outfit, despite the fact that my parents had asked me to eat first and get dressed up later. The excitement I had inside me would not let me listen. I sat down in my brand-new dress that my mum had bought me for my most-special-birthday-ever and dug into my fruit loops with chocolate milk. I was talking with mounting excitement to my mum about who was coming to my birthday party and was completely absorbed in my thoughts about the amazing day I had ahead of me. And then it happened. To my horror, my cereal spilled all over my new dress.

And yes—as you may have guessed from the melodrama of the story—my birthday was totally ruined.

Now surely you wouldn't think spilling a bit of cereal on my dress should ruin my birthday, right? I mean, couldn't I just get changed into a different outfit and carry on with my day?

Wrong.

As I said, in mine, and most other people's childhoods, there were no shades of grey. Life was either good or bad, happy or sad. And at that moment, with chocolate milk and fruit loops sinking into my beautiful birthday dress, I was sad.

That was until my dad came over to help me clean up. I was expecting him to lecture me. To say, 'I told you so,' and that I should have listened to my mum's suggestion to not put my new dress on until I was done with breakfast.

Instead, he looked at me with a loving glimmer in his eyes and amidst my tears, he asked me to smile.

I was shocked. I was downright offended. The nerve of my dad! Asking me to smile when my birthday was clearly ruined? Had he lost his mind? It wasn't what I had expected to hear, and I had no intention of smiling.

Something to know about my dad is that he was always a joker, and if he could make light of a situation, then he would.

"Go on, smile princess," he repeated, making a silly face and reaching down to wipe off my tears. Very stubbornly, with my arms crossed and an 'I'm not having any of this' attitude, I forced a very fake smile on to my miserable, pouty face.

He laughed at my expression, which actually made me more frustrated! And he said, "there, see? You're all better."

I didn't understand. I responded in frustration that I wasn't feeling better at all, but he said, "you smiled, even though you were feeling sad! That's one little step to making your day better, and now, sweetheart, the next smile will be easier."

Then my dad gave me a huge grin and I squished up my face, trying hard to stay mad, but I couldn't and so I started to laugh. He was right, I did feel better.

Now let's go back to the number line.

We have been made to think only numbers to the right side are 'positive', but the truth is that

every movement to the right, irrespective of where you are on the line, is positive.

Positivity is not just about moving from zero to five on that scale. It's about *any* movement in the *right* direction. A lot of the time it isn't that easy to just zip ahead and be a five. It takes work, and we must give ourselves credit for that.

You can start by appreciating the little wins that happen all the time. I'm a firm believer in that you can't have a bad day, week, or year, because there must have been SOMETHING that was good. Did you have water to drink? Food to eat? Was it sunny?

I believe in being grateful for the little things, because those are really the big things, and everything else is just static. So, if you're able to turn a negative day, week, or year around in a split-second decision, great!

But maybe you aren't one of those people who can turn a terrible, awful day around. Maybe it takes more time for you. Maybe you actually got mad at me when just now when I said that you can't have a 'bad day' because you've had the worst of luck your entire life!

Yet deep down, perhaps you realize you have a bit of work to do on YOU. A little more self-love and acceptance before you leap up to a five, and that is just fine.

Let me just tell you this: You are perfect where you are right now, because where you are right now is reading this book, and that means you've made the conscious decision to look for a way to lead a more positive life. Jumping from a zero to a five is monumental. But positivity still applies and is more of a milestone when we move from say, a -5 to -3.

THAT IS PROGRESS!

Positivity is when you feel pleasant often enough that you can ward off negative feelings.

The more positive you feel, the more positive you become.

Throughout this book, you will be learning to take little steps that all lead to the ultimate goal of mastering your mindset and homing in on your inner magic.

We will be moving closer to a better life each day, and as we repeat these steps over and over again, it will become our nature to be positive. To respond to life with our positive mindset first.

We will abstain from negativity. We will remove from ourselves, and our surroundings, these awful, dream-killing things like pessimism and fear, and we will sprinkle in the good stuff, like optimism and hope.

We are not the first to go down this path in search of a better way of living, and we will in no way be the last. Others have had this experience, this longing for a better way, a brighter path. For success and wealth, health and happiness. Through my studies and over a decade of experience I have learned the best techniques and curated them here for you in this book.

Thomas Edison went through a world of failure in his quest to create the light bulb. For a long time, no matter what he tried, it wouldn't work! In fact, it took him a year of studies and many failed attempts to even bring the idea to fruition, let alone get it functioning.

In the end, because he stayed positive and confident of his desired outcome, he brought it life. His first lightbulb stayed lit for 13.5 hours successfully.

This is why he said:

"I have not failed. I've just found 10,000 ways that won't work!
Genius is 1% inspiration and 99% perspiration."
-Thomas Edison

It will be said over and over in this book that the choice to stay positive is up to you. The choice to actually utilize these steps to change your mindset, and therein change your life, is entirely up to you.

Nobody can beat positivity into another person. It cannot be forced and trust me: I have tried and failed! It just doesn't work that way. You cannot decide for another person that it is time for them to be more positive. That it's time for them to change their lives for the better. That is their decision and theirs alone.

A person gets to the point where they realize that it costs nothing to be positive (and, hey! It makes them feel good too!) and it takes a whole lot more will power to stay negative.

It's actually a challenge to stay gloomy, negative and talk bad about every good thing you see. It's exhausting.

So, I am going to encourage you to make the choice today. To make that choice for yourself, and forget about anyone else's prerogatives.

Choose to stay positive no matter how hard it may seem at the moment. Because if we can smile once today, we will be able to smile twice tomorrow, and before long we will forget what it feels like not to smile.

So put your positive pants on, and let's do this!

"Whether you believe you can do a thing or not,
you are absolutely right."
-Henry Ford

THE TWO POLES

My father was right. The next time something happened that made me feel sad, all he had to do was show up, tell me to smile, and I would. After a while, all he would do was show up, make a silly face and I would smile.

Then after that, when I was alone, I would just imagine what he told me and would laugh about how silly it was to be upset over such a little thing. And guess what? I would smile.

When I was a bit older, my father explained to me something called polarity. Polarity deals with balance: hot and cold, east and west, up and down, that kind of thing. In chemistry, polarity refers to a way in which atoms bond together. Polarity in our own subconscious is different.

My father explained," if you want to live positively, and stay perpetually in that positivity, you must understand the two poles of mind.

"But before I tell you about these poles," he started, "I want you to know that they are all the same thing; just in varying degrees."

I was already slightly confused, but thought 'what the heck', and listened to what he was explaining.

"And because they are all the same thing," he continued," it is within your ability to 'tune the dial' to the degree of your own choosing. What will make you happy versus what may make you sad," my father said as he made a hand motion of turning a small dial up and down.

I stared blankly at his face, scrunched up my nose and said, "what?".

Eventually what he meant became clear to me, so here is where I will explain to you what this means for us as we journey down a path of self-awareness and mastery of our mindset.

Imagine a thermometer. Close your eyes for a second and see a thermometer in your mind's eye.

I'll wait.

This device called a thermometer only records temperature. Or, maybe I should say, it only records varying degrees of temperature. So, whether you call it hot or cold, it is temperature and nothing else.

Now, what does the mind measure in varying degrees? What is it you control that you can 'tune' to your choosing?

The answer is simple: our emotions!

Fun fact: the word 'emotion' can be translated to mean Energy-In-Motion. This means that our emotions are literally our energy—they strengthen or weaken us.

And whether you call them emotions or feelings, the point remains the same: OUR FEELINGS ARE TOTALLY WITHIN OUR CONTROL.

There is a neutral state—let's call it zero—where we are just okay, or 'meh, nothing special'. Then there is everything to the left of zero, the negative zone. Here is where you find hate, fear, depression, envy, guilt, anxiety... Negative emotions.

When we are in this zone, we respond in kind. We criticize, we are impatient, and we are pessimistic. We tune the dial down and we realize that we become heavy, unproductive and unfocused. Then there is the right side of the emotional line. Fortunately for us, this side has no end! It is the side the dial that produces hope, joy, enthusiasm, excitement, happiness, optimism, love... you name it.

It is that side which makes us light and appreciative. This side keeps us expecting good things, irrespective of the present situation. This side is the inspiration behind every smile...and every happy moment in our lives.

The good news is this: every time you tune the dial up, even in its most infinitesimal measure, you move up the positive line. And remembering this simple fact greatly improves your emotional control, as well as your ability to feel good. You start to see how simple it can be to change your mood to happy, like by smiling or laughing instead of scowling.

"There are three things that cannot be long hidden.
The sun, the moon, and the truth."
-Buddha

While discussing the mind, it is important to state that there are two which we should know about. The first being the conscious mind and the other being the subconscious.

The conscious mind dominates us in our waking state. It consists of five senses with which we communicate with the physical world. Those senses are sight, smell, touch, hearing and taste. The brain presides over these senses and when they are working in good condition, we interact with the outside world effectively. The conscious mind helps us learn new things because it can identify and contrast between one thing and another.

The subconscious mind handles things that are beyond our conscious control. These are things like breathing, blood pumping and heart rate. Our imaginations, dreams and thoughts (whether negative or positive) are also the domain of the subconscious mind.

It works without effort; it moves as such that there can be no failure. For if there is a failure, the entire system will crumble. And its effortlessness is evident in every breath you take during sleep.

Now, let's look at the example of playing the piano. To do so with ease requires both the conscious and subconscious minds to work together.

The beginning of the learning process is difficult. We have to look at the keys before we strike. We strain to recall which sequence the music is playing in. Our hand muscles will hurt because we are not accustomed to that kind of activity. And it is all done with conscious effort. However, after constant practice, we realize that we don't have to look at the keys as often as before. That our hands know where to go without our conscious activity.

Through diligent practice, we will learn how to play beautifully, and one day can play the piano while having a conversation with a friend or teaching someone else the skill.

Therefore, we need both minds. The subconscious works without supervision, but we need the conscious in order to direct the subconscious on what objectives to follow.

This synchronization of both minds working together has accomplished such great feats as the telephone, the airplane, the wonderful compositions of Bach, timeless paintings, incredible stories… and so much more.

"Whatever we plant in our subconscious mind and nourish with repetition and emotion will one day become reality."
-Earl Nightingale

EMOTIONAL INTELLIGENCE

Emotional Intelligence, or EQ, is the understanding of emotions, ours and others, and the appropriate labeling and placing of these emotions to better understand ourselves and increase our social skills and productivity.

EQ shows us all we need to know about the powerful tool we call emotions and how to creatively and effectively harness this energy that is constantly in motion.

EQ is further broken down into different parts:

- **Self-Awareness:** This deals with you, the individual, understanding your emotions or moods and knowing how they affect others in your circle.
- **Self-Regulation:** This deals with your ability to hold and scrutinize every feeling so as to redirect negative

energy into more positive ones. Mastering self-regulation is a study of control.

- **Motivation:** Wanting to do something not because of the financial gratification but because of an inward drive. On the road to living positively, obstacles will naturally appear. It is our inner motivation that helps us move past the blocks in our path. We learn to generate our inner strength and inspiration in order to push forward.

- **Social Skills:** This focuses on how you relate to others; how well do you manage relationships? What are your thoughts on building networks? How do you communicate what you feel with others? The answers to these questions determine where you are in terms of social skills.

- **Empathy:** This is the understanding of someone else's emotions. It is often confused with sympathy but differs in that sympathy deals with feeling sorry for another person's misfortune, while empathy encompasses all emotions, and how we relate to them.

- **Stress Management:** This is the way in which we deal with the various stresses and stressors that we are faced with in our day to day lives. Due to the insidious nature of stress, we can find ourselves on the negative side of the line before we even realize that we were moving towards the left. Therefore, it is of the utmost importance that we learn how to recognize and then manage stress as we come across it.

By managing our emotions, we can manage our lives. We become better, and we understand ourselves more.

We begin to embrace our inner magic and take control of our desires, creating that perfect harmony between our dreams and what we can make reality.

"Worship whichever gods if you must, but your first duty should be to understand who and what you are. Man! Know thyself."
-Socrates

THE POWER

"Positive thinking will let you do everything better than negative thinking ever could."
-Zig Ziglar

When I was young, I had a temper issue. If I wanted something, I would ask nicely… But just once. After that, I asked through shouting and tears, with a pounding heart and anxiety going through the roof—as you can imagine, this was not fun for my parents.

I was told by my mum that it's a whole lot more productive to be gentle in my approach, and that being harsh would get me nothing. She remained steadfast in teaching me this lesson. When I acted like a total brat… I got nothing. I didn't understand this until she told me the following story, which highlighted the significance of being calm, positive and emotionally collected.

One day the sun and the wind were feeling a bit bored. After debating on what to do in order to make their day interesting, they decided to have a bet. They said they would have a contest to see who was more persuasive.

After looking for a suitable way to test their skills, they fixed their eyes on a man who was walking past. He was fully dressed, and he wore a suit jacket. They made a wager that the one who could get the man to remove his jacket would be the winner. This was agreed upon by both parties, and the wind went first.

The wind started small and what the man felt was the environment getting windy. He was apprehensive and he started moving more quickly. Seeing this, the wind came harder; thinking that his harshness would forcefully remove the jacket from the man's body.

This didn't work as the man held on tighter to his jacket, and he brought out his umbrella because he thought the rains would come down any moment. He continued, holding his jacket even tighter as the wind became very fierce.

After minutes of torture, the wind gave up. It knew there was no way he was getting that jacket off. It was virtually impossible because the man had buttoned it up to the fullest.

Then the sun decided to try. He, like the wind, started calmly. The wind didn't see how the sun was going to do it. The wind though that surely the sun was calm and made no noise, so how would he get someone to take off his jacket?

But the sun had a plan. He started to warm the place up and the man naturally, started to feel hot in the jacket. The sun increased the temperature a bit and the man removed a button. At this point the wind knew it had lost already. The sun kept going up till the man was sweating and had to take off the jacket completely. The sun prevailed through calmer, better planned tactics.

What we can take from this story is that while force has become the societal convention, acting from a place of positivity and calmness will yield better results. We need to unlearn what we think we know and then we must understand that in the long run, being calm will solve all issues and overcome all challenges.

Positivity has the power to help you accomplish this. By mastering your mindset to put forth positive emotions and thoughts first, you can learn how to unleash the hidden store of magic that lies within you.

It takes time to re-learn how to think, to change what can be years of negative thought patterns. Think of it as an emotional investment for your mental health.

And oh, what a great investment it is!

> *"Every moment of one's existence, one is growing into more or retreating into less."*
> *-Norman Mailer*

STEP ONE

ACCEPTANCE

"Happiness can only exist in acceptance."
-George Orwell

It is said that acceptance is the last stage of grief. That is true. But what is truer is that

ACCEPTANCE IS THE FIRST STAGE OF A NEW LIFE.

Own it. Accept who you are. Accept that the person you have become is a result of everything that has happened in your past. That is where we begin in living the life we have always wanted.

But who are you? In order to do this, we must go into, and examine the past.

I don't remember the day I was born, most of us don't. But what I do know is this: I was born without fear, without hate. I had no envy of others and I wasn't critical of others. I was just me, as perfect as a newborn baby is. Happy as a clam.

I had no worries… I WAS AWESOME.

And you know what? The same goes for every person ever born.

We are all born positive. And as we grow and become toddlers, then little kids, we understand how to go for what we want. We say what we feel, and we don't know how to harbor long-lasting negative emotions.

But we all start to lose our awesomeness at some point. The more we grow up, the more negative events happen and the more emotionally guarded we become. Better put, we start to lose the manifestation of our awesomeness.

Our inner magic started getting cluttered up with newfound emotions that affected us.

We start to see limitation in one way or another, we start to believe statements like:

- Not every day is Christmas day.
- You can't have your cake and eat it too.
- You can't always get what you want.
- You have to choose between happiness and wealth.
- You can't win them all.

These statements suggest that you can't be in the 'positive' zone all the time.

Life Story:

Jerome was a fairly happy and normal kid. He was bold and playful. He loved military toys like action figures, armored cars, and toy guns; he was lucky because his father could afford to buy him the cool toys he liked playing with.

Life was good. In fact, it was beautiful and exciting. But all that changed in the months after his dad lost all his money in an investment-gone-south.

Jerome noticed that his father became increasingly grouchy. Things which were jokes in the house before no longer were taken as such.

His dad became an angry person with a temper that was very out of character.

New terms were introduced to the man's speech. Questions like "Do I look like I am made of money?" became a regularity when Jerome would talk about a toy he wanted. Gradually, Jerome stopped asking for things from his dad. He became closed off, and who can blame him? He was only nine years old when things turned bad for his father's fortune.

Jerome grew up believing that he can't always get what he wants. Worse, he believed he may be offending someone if he even asked for something that he wanted. This progressed over the years, and these beliefs aided in turning Jerome to a terrible receiver. When he would be given gifts from his friends, he would say things like "I hope it wasn't stressful getting me this," and "you shouldn't have."

It wasn't until Jerome met his wife, Karen, that he was taught the value of acceptance. The more of her love he accepted, the more he began to discover what had gone wrong in his past, and he begin work to fix it.

Over the course of our lives, we have learned fear and negative thinking. Even if we don't recall those fears or thoughts, we began accepting them as our reality.

We have learned to hoard things instead of emotions to fill the void that has been left by the same lessons that taught Jerome to be a terrible receiver. We believe that we don't deserve to accept the gifts that life delivers us, so we hold tighter to find that same fulfilment in material things because we feel that there just isn't enough. Which is truly the opposite of what we should be doing. We should be freely giving so that we can welcome MORE into our lives.

If you have only $5 left in your bank account, give $2 to charity at the checkout till when they ask. Money isn't yours, and the more freely you give it, the more freely it will come floating into your life... like magic.

We have accepted ideas which encouraged our negativity, and gradually, we slowly began to cover up and bury our own inner magic.

And somewhere along the way, we have stopped knowing that we are awesome.

Note: I didn't say we stopped knowing we were awesome.

I said,

"We stopped knowing that we ARE awesome."

Let's learn from two of my favorite materials:

GOLD: This is one of the most, if not the single most valued of all precious metals. It has been revered for centuries across cultures and countries. There are stories originating in ancient Greece of an alien race which came to earth looking for this precious metal.

We know all the idioms that prove the value of gold, such as, "Heaven has its streets paved in gold," and "as precious as gold," as well as "a heart of gold." And so, we know that gold is a lovely thing we all want to have.

But did it always glimmer like that? No. Gold in its natural form is not what you would expect. In its natural form it looks duller, often covered up by pieces of rock and debris. Yet that does not stop it from being what it is. That does not in any way reduce its value.

DIAMOND: Though people would kill to have these, in their natural state no one would look at them twice. They are black, shapeless, and they don't have that vibrance that attracts us to them. But when their inner beauty is coaxed out through shaping and polishing, they become something valuable.

This precious stone is so sought after that many diamonds can be tracked through the trail of blood left in their wake. Yet that does not stop it from being what it is. That doesn't stop the bright, magical shine of a diamond.

That is why I say that,

You Are Awesome.

Irrespective of the state a diamond is in before it is polished, it knows that it is a diamond... It knows that it is still the hardest substance known to man and that only another diamond can cut it. Even if no one else does, the diamond knows. Same way that gold knows it is gold.

The same way that you need to know how awesome, amazing and magical you truly are.

I'm going to lay it out for you here, nice and simple. You must accept that there is something special about you. Even if right now, wherever you are in life, you feel that you are 'unpolished' and 'uncut'. Like a rough diamond disguised as a rock.

Whatever happened in the past, be it your fault or not; whatever it is that clouded your shine, maybe even buried it, you must know your light was never extinguished. And guess what? It can never be. That is the magic of it.

You begin by saying to yourself,

"Irrespective of the past, I AM AWESOME."

Make this your mantra and say it every day—even when you don't believe it. Say it until you begin to believe it and really feel that you are awesome, because you are. And just like that— perhaps with a little effort at first—this thought will begin to uncover the awesomeness somewhere within you. It will stir back up that inner you who knows there's a whole lot of awesome inside.

Your mind is your vessel to guide, and you use it to control the outcomes in life. You are awesome, so decide you are awesome. Tell yourself you are awesome. Say it out loud right now.

Good! Now say it again.

Repeat it over and over until you feel it in your chest and your blood. Feel your awesomeness flowing through your veins with each pump of your awesome heart.

It's worth repeating,

"Irrespective of the past, I AM AWESOME."

Life Story:

Clara started to forget her awesomeness when she first started dating. Everything always seemed to start out fine when Clara first got into a new relationship.

She would meet someone who seemed amazing, and they would spend more and more time together going on dates and having fun.

Then it always seemed to start to turn sour. She noticed her partners pulling away from her, and she felt that the relationship was falling to pieces as she began to pick her partners apart. The more time that she spent with them, the more she began noticing flaws that they had, or red flags that would pop up more frequently. She started feeling that she had a terrible selection in partners, and that was why she ended up heartbroken and hurt so often, never having successful, happy, lasting relationships.

Clara would always blame each issue on the new partner. He was either on the phone all the time, or he forgot her birthday. He looked at another lady in a suspicious manner, or he wasn't giving her the affection she needed. It was one issue after the other until each relationship ended.

She never for once thought to check if, for any reason, the problem may have come from her. Clara went on for years, and through many failed relationships, not understanding that her problems could be of her own making.

She didn't think to search back her own history to see if there was a fault in her actions and reactions at any time.

She developed her own beliefs which she accepted such as:

Men cheat

Men are forgetful

Men are not sensitive

Because she believed her own truths, her relationships kept manifesting them. That is to say that her negative thought patterns always supplied her with the answers she was looking for. For example, she assumed he would cheat, and so any behaviour— whether real or contrived—that gave evidence to his adulterous nature would substantiate and reinforce her beliefs. Then she would carry that 'truth' into her next relationship, and once again it would become her reality. A toxic self-fulfilling prophecy.

Sounds terrible right? Would you want to live a life never trusting your partner and slowly destroying every relationship you're in?

Does anyone really want to live their life in constant fear of how other people are going to maybe/possibly affect our lives? It's not healthy to pre-judge people based on one bad event that happened in your life.

We want to focus on seeing the GOOD in everything, including our relationships. This is not to say that you should overlook when something is really making you uncomfortable, or when something doesn't 'click'.

Always follow your instincts, but remember that our preconceived notions can shape what, and how we see people. Our 'truths' can make or break how we feel about someone.

Remember that you are more likely to draw people into your life who will treat you badly if you are constantly thinking that people will treat you badly! That's a sure-fire way to block good people from entering your life.

Project positivity. Let go of the bad events that happened to you. They are in the past and by refusing to LET THEM GO, you are dragging those same events into your present.

Live with an abundance of positive energy and you will manifest the best relationship of your life. Trust in the magic within yourself.

> *"We don't see things as they are;*
> *we see them as we are."*
> *-Anais*

Are you in love with yourself?

Part of acceptance is learning to be comfortable being you.

No one knows you better than you know yourself. Be content accepting that. You are the best you can be at this point and when you choose to be better, it is up to you, and only you, to effect that change.

Being comfortable means that you have confidence in who you are and your inner abilities.

It means knowing that you are in charge and you cannot go wrong. It means accepting the fact that all things work together for your good. That because you are awesome, you can only attract awesomeness.

Life Story:

Suzanne is an American teenager who has lived in Europe since a very young age. She has always been on the bigger side and she would quite often be teased while she was growing up. She was what some people would define as overweight in our body-shaming society.

She didn't want anyone to know it got to her, so she would put up a straight face and go about her usual business. She was made to believe by her schoolmates that her clothes didn't look good on her. That she needed to watch what she ate and how she ate it.

Though she was born in Wisconsin, her father had been transferred to work in Europe and she had been there pretty much all her life.

Upon graduating high school, Suzanne had the opportunity to return to the United States for her college education. When she arrived, she realized she wasn't fat. She saw the massive obesity crisis in America and it became clear to her that she was actually quite healthy compared to many of her peers.

It was a stigma of one culture that had affected her mindset on how her body felt.

All of a sudden, a confidence she had never felt come upon her. She thought to herself, "Why did I let all those kids in high school make me feel bad about myself?" She went into a store and her sizes of clothes were readily available, it was like magic to her.

Suzanne did some research and quickly realized that the sizing in Europe was much different than in America. She realized that there were heavier people in general in the USA than there were in Europe, and that she wasn't actually overweight.

She fell in love with the way she looked and decided that no one was ever going to make her feel less than the awesome lady she is.

Who wouldn't want to be more like Suzanne? We want to fill ourselves with confidence and self-acceptance, shaking out of the boundaries that have been set up by the society we live in.

We have to realize that this life is OURS, therefore we must embrace who we are and focus on creating and manifesting a better life for ourselves. This begins when you free yourself from the standards and segregations installed in our minds from a young age.

It's not up to other people to tell us how our bodies should be. Not how we should look, or how we should feel. It is up to us to decide for ourselves what makes us feel good, healthy and happy.

Your goal in life should be to become healthy from the inside out. This includes your emotional wellbeing, not just how your clothes fit. Allowing others to make you feel a certain way can be damaging.

Make healthy choices and feel good about yourself.

Shut out and distance yourself from the nay-sayers and the judgmental peers that make you feel any less fabulous than you truly are.

Be you, be free and be happy. You have a lot to be grateful for and a lot of love to give. So, let your magic shine.

Practice Your Power Exercise: (*you need a partner for this*)

Raise your right hand and say to yourself, "I AM WEAK" ten times. Then get your partner to try to push your hand down. As he/she is pushing down, try to keep it up.

How did you do?

Now repeat the same exercise. Only this time, repeat the words, "I AM AWESOME."

You will find that it is a whole lot harder for your partner to push your hand down.

This is the power of acceptance and, more importantly, believing the truth.

And as you accept this truth, you can say goodbye to grief and welcome the new phase of life.

> *"Real people make mistakes;*
> *happy people accept that."*
> *-Anonymous*

STEP TWO

KNOWLEDGE

"The sum of all our knowledge is directly related to our reaction towards our personal experiences in life and how we choose to learn from them."
-Sarah Hall

Knowledge is power. With the knowledge shared in this chapter, you will have the ability to decide exactly how any given situation will affect you.

If you go to a brain surgeon about a pain in your knee, he will probably look at your brain to determine the source of the problem. You know why? Because that is the area in which he is knowledgeable. This is how it is with everything else.

If you talk to a Feng Shui expert about money problems, she will first look at how you arrange your room. That is her area of expertise.

So, what is my implication here? What do I mean about knowledge?

We want to know the answers in life so that we can better act and react to any given situation.

What is it specifically that we want to know?

We want to know the truth. And what is the truth?

The truth can be anything that sets us free from the negative side of the line that I showed you in the first chapter. The truth is anything that keeps us from sliding to that dark and dreary left side of the number zero. And the truth is different for everyone.

Have you ever heard something that made sense even though you don't remember ever hearing it before?

An example of that is this: "Life was meant to be abundant."

How does that phrase feel? It gives us a little more hope. And hope is on the positive side of the line. It has a positive polarity.

However, for many of us, there seems to be a lack in evidence that would prove that life truly was meant to be abundant. So many people are trapped in a negative mindset. Trapped in their past and trapped in thinking the worst can happen at any given time.

What those people don't understand is that to create abundance in your life, you must open your heart, your arms and your spirit to abundance.

You must be grateful for what you already have. You must cast a vision of yourself living the life you desire.

If you've never practised this way of thinking and living before, it can seem like a really difficult task to begin filling your mind with optimism instead of the constant worry that was your mental chatter before.

Negative thoughts will always creep back, and that's OK! But it's our job to say, "No thank you, negative thought." And instead send a positive thought to take its place.

This is the reason that people struggle so hard with abundance and accepting that there is more to life than where they are at right now.

Life story:

A lady named Tabitha grew up believing that all men cheated on women. She had accepted this as the truth because she lived with an abusive dad, who had cheated on her mother many times. She grew up watching their abusive relationship and believed that was how romantic relationships ended up.

Now, we all know that there are good men out there who don't cheat on their wives, but Tabitha did not know this.

She believed a lie... and it became her truth. What this did to Tabitha was that it made her worried, alone and unhappy.

She avoided getting into long term commitments, even though she desired to have a happy relationship one day.

You see, deep down she believed that all men were like her father and that eventually, when she too would get married, her husband would cheat, and they would fight endlessly.

As she grew up, Tabitha began a stable career and was making good money. She opted to be independent and started to tell anyone who asked that she had no interest in marriage.

Every time she got into a new relationship; she would always end up pushing the men away. She didn't realize what had become of her.

53

That's where many of us are in life. It's unfortunate, but it's true. And it's not our fault because WE JUST DON'T KNOW!

Yet what makes it worse is that we think we know, don't we? We think we know everything, so we don't want to hear another point of view.

Have you ever been talking to someone and their response to everything you tell them is some variation of, "Oh, I know."

Isn't that frustrating? Is that person YOU?!

STOP IT.

This mentality of thinking we know everything actually keeps us moving leftward on the scale, towards negativity. And that, my friends, is what we need to overcome.

Once you can overcome your own mind, and learn to control your thoughts, you can begin to change your life. Begin by accepting that there is much you do not know.

Imagine that you have a cup, and that cup is full of water—teeming to the brim. Now imagine you want to add more to that cup. Is it going to fit? No, it's not. Because your cup is full. Only when you dump out some of that old, stagnant water, can you fit more into your cup.

This is the same way that knowledge works. If you already think you know everything there is to know, then you don't have room for new knowledge to come into your life. You're missing out. Big time.

So now it's time to dump out your cup.

Throw out the words, "I know."

Change your mindset to one of constant awe, and learning, and watch the flood of opportunity come your way.

Accept that there is a whole universe of possibilities, and that there is no way that one single person could ever know everything there is to know. Then learn to let go of your ego, by releasing one negative thought at a time.

> *"A wise man knows nothing."*
> *-Buddha*

Why do you think Buddha said this? He certainly did not mean that we don't actually truly know anything at all.

What he meant is that a wise man knows nothing, therefore he is opening the door for the opportunity to constantly be able to learn new ideas, new concepts and new information.

When we think we know everything about everything, it actually takes away from what we can learn about life. It stops us from moving forwards. It keeps us trapped in the negative zone.

Weigh every idea upon your own inner dial before you accept it. If it makes you feel heavy, then understand that you are moving to negativity, so let it go.

If someone comes to you with an idea, and your ego tells you "I know all about that." Stop yourself. Allow yourself to hear their idea with an open mind, because who knows how far it will take you?

If you weigh it and it makes you feel light, accept it as truth and live as though that is the truth for you. This may be very hard for you to do at first, especially if you have a big, strong, passionate ego like me! But take one step at a time and keep catching and forcing yourself to let go of your desire to already know the best for everything.

That's what the saying 'fake it until you make it' means.

Because with each new time you practice this, although it may feel "fake" to your ego, you are becoming internally wiser. You are growing.

The following would be the case if positive inner knowledge was involved in Tabitha's life:

Tabitha would have recognized that the idea of all men being cheaters was false because it made her feel emotionally "heavy". She would have proceeded to reason the truth for herself—all men can't possibly be like that.

Then with that truth (the knowledge that there are good men in the world) she would have acted in such a manner as to attract GOOD men, ignoring every terrible man that she came across.

I encourage you to read more books, journals, and studies to expand your knowledge. I like to think of this as going to the 'Spirit Gym' for a mental workout. You can do something every day that broadens your knowledge.

Whether you have to download self-help audio books and listen to them in your car—as I did for ages while I was working as an insurance broker—or whether you can read at home in your downtime, just get started.

As you start to expand your spiritual knowledge, you will begin to attract the lifestyle you desire towards you.

Do not limit yourself to your field of knowledge, or to your favorite genre. People tend to make this mistake when they're just starting out on the whole personal growth journey. If there's a book that sounds like you would never read it, give it a try.

It might be about something that sounds totally hocus pocus to you, like 'The Secret'. Or maybe it's a book about leadership, but you've been a follower your whole life. Whatever it is, read it.

Experiment with different foods, different cultures, meet new people and learn from them.

Have you ever heard that life begins outside your comfort zone? It truly does. So, broaden that zone by eliminating it entirely.

When you do something new, something exciting, something that maybe even scares you; it changes you. Your adrenaline starts pumping, your heart beats faster, you experience new thoughts and a rush of power and confidence within yourself.

Get out there!

Start DOING and LIVING.

Don't waste any more time procrastinating!

Take it from me, I wasted far too many years of my life on bad choices, bad boyfriends and bad friendships. So much time lost dwelling on the past and focusing on things I could never change. This is a form of true personal torture!

Just save yourself now and LET IT GO. Let it all go. It can be hard at first, but if you want the new, amazing, kick-ass lifestyle you've always dreamed of having… then you'll find a way to get through those days when it feels like you can't let it go. You can do it. I believe in you.

If you are able to afford it, travel and learn about different cultures. If you currently cannot afford to travel, then pick out a place you've always wanted to go and cut out a photo from a magazine of it, or print one off from online, then stick that photo right on your dream board.

You know what? Take it a step further. Tape that photo to the roof in your bedroom, right above where you lay your head to rest every night. Then each night you will fall asleep thinking about it, envisioning it, making it happen through the power of your own thoughts.

Envision yourself packing your bags, getting on the plane, taking off and landing in that tropical paradise you've always dream of. Envision the heat on your skin and the sand beneath your feet. FEEL IT. And the universe will put the means to get there into your path. It's the purest form of inner magic we are privy to.

I've done it. You can do it too.

Anyone can do anything they set their minds to.

I honestly believe that is the truth. And in my experience, I have seen it happen to countless people. People who, at one point in their lives, thought that they could never do anything.

Yet they made the conscious decision to change their way of thought, and now they are successful and able to reach further and go farther every day.

All this happened because they found their Magic and they unleashed it. One day at a time. One thought at a time.

Increase your knowledge base so that you may be of help to more people. So that you too can share your knowledge with others and be a positive spark of magic to guide someone else through their foggy path. Be constantly learning and growing by accepting that there is so much to learn and so much growth to be had in this life. There is always something more to know.

How do you know that you know something? You truly know that you know something only once you have tried and re-tried it under controlled circumstances. When you can successfully replicate your results at will.

How do you know that fire burns? Because you have probably experienced it firsthand as a child or as an adult... or both. The results were the same in all situations and then you saw that it was fact.

Fire burns!

This is where knowledge trumps blind belief.

Children are usually told by their parents that swallowing the seeds of fruits, such as oranges, would cause the seed to germinate inside their stomachs and the leaves would grow out from their ears and head. Of course, this is a ploy by the parents so as to ensure that children don't swallow seeds.

However, every child soon discovers the truth because let us face it… It is very hard to enjoy good fruit and not let a seed or two slip through the throat mistakenly.

What usually happens is that once the seed slips through, the child, full of fear, waits for the seed to germinate and then... it doesn't.

Some children would run to their parents and tell them what happened, and the parents could say they have done something to remedy the situation. Something to prevent the seed from growing in their belly, and then they tell the child to make sure it doesn't happen again. Whichever the case, eventually knowledge kicks in and we realize that seeds don't germinate in the stomach.

Such knowledge starts to take root in elementary science class when we hear that seeds need a certain kind of condition in order to grow.

We soon discover that those conditions do not exist in our stomachs in any way… That it is virtually impossible to have seeds germinate in our stomachs.

With this knowledge comes confidence, and with confidence our fear is expunged.

That is another reason we should continue to learn. The more truth we know, the less afraid we are. And, the last time I checked, fear was on the left side of our line.

> *"Let go of fear and make more room for the magical stuff, like love and acceptance."*
> *-Sarah Hall*

Our world is rife with pressures and triggers that try to keep us ignorant and fearful. Every day we are reminded on the news of terrorists who are trying to kill us and because of that our calls have to be monitored.

Personally, I never watch the news. Not in years. I mean YEARS. I find the news stations stressful, upsetting and it fills my minds with negativity that I do not need, and has no relation to my path in life.

If you are a stock broker, then set aside time to listen to the stock news, because that is part of your life. But shut out the rest of that mental noise.

It's more destructive than you know.

We are reminded of all sorts of diseases and illness that you might catch, and that in turn keeps us faithful customers to the pharmaceutical companies...

We are bombarded with harsh economic 'realities' and predictions, which keep us working at a job we don't find fulfillment in, just because "it's a harsh world out there" and "you won't find anything better."

Has anyone ever doubted your capabilities? Doubted your ideas? Your ambitions? Has someone told you that it's almost impossible to get rich, publish a book, climb Mount Everest?

Truth Bomb: That's their own unhappiness with their own lives that they're projecting onto you.

Those negative statements that we may have been told as we're growing up, or that surround our lives now, can be very toxic to our growth and mastering our mindset.

These web of lies quickly fall of from us when we realize such truths as:

- Water and fruits are the best medicine we could ever come across.
- We can never be unsafe in our life path if our thoughts are in the right place.
- Fear is a leading cause of death.

When we KNOW these truths, and allow ourselves to believe what is true for us (as opposed to popular opinion), then we can really start to grow into our most amazing selves.

We all have different truths we believe, and breaking down the buildup of what has been projected onto us throughout our lives allows us to create our own truths.

That is the power of knowledge.

Practice Your Power Exercise:

Think of negative statements you have believed or said in the past. Write down as many as you can remember. Then leave it overnight.

The next day come back to that paper and write the opposites of what was written down before—no matter how crazy they may sound.

Now, take time and study these new sentences and beliefs. How do they make you feel?

STEP THREE

DESIRE

"Your burning desire to change your life must be greater than your fears of how you're going to achieve those changes and transform your life."
-Sarah Hall

Ultimately, to live positively, you must know what it is you want. And you must allow yourself to want it.

Here in this chapter I am going to explain the difference between wanting something and being desperate for something. There is a really big difference between the two, and when desperation rules, you are more likely to get the opposite of what you desire.

When you want something, you, by default, start to imagine what having it would mean to you. You begin to think about how it's going to benefit your life once you get it, and the best part is, you feel good about what you want. And because of the way you feel about it, you start seeing your desire around you.

For example, when I was fantasising about my new car, I started seeing BMW's everywhere. Literally everywhere. I remember thinking, "Are there always this many BMW's around...? Maybe they had a sale or something!"

Surely you have experienced this before. Yes, you did it without knowing what you were doing, and that is the wonderful thing about this magical form of visualization.

We can all do it.

The tricky part is this: What happens if you don't get what you want? Because as you know, you might not always get what you want… at least not right away!

This is the thin line between wanting something and being desperate.

When you genuinely want something, you should be fine whether or not you get it.

Your mindset should be something like this:

"I would really like to get this thing, but if for some reason I don't get it right now, that is still okay."

Desperate thoughts go more like this:

"I don't know what I would do if I don't get what I want."

See the difference?

Life Story:

A friend of mine once shared an experience he had with his daughter. She wanted a dog, and the first thing she did was ask her father to get her a dog. He refused to get it, telling her that dogs were more responsibility than she was to ready to take on. Naturally, she didn't let that stop her. When she asked and saw that her dad wouldn't budge, she started asking her mum. Again, mum didn't seem to understand how much she wanted the dog.

So, what did the little girl do? She didn't go to steal a dog, she made up one. She created an invisible dog and even gave him a name. Her goal was to get her parents to see that she could be responsible enough to care for one.

Unfortunately, her parents still didn't get her one. The little girl started drawing pictures of her dog everywhere. On all her books there were pictures of the dog. All her assignments from school had one answer, the picture of her dog. And, of course, all the walls in the house became canvas for her newly found art passion—her dog. Still the dog didn't come around.

One day in school she went to the lost and found corner and she saw a dog collar. She picked it up and brought it home. She told her parents it was for her dog.

After a while, a new neighbor moved in and he had a dog. The little girl became instant best friends with the family, and she would always be at their house after school to play with the dog.

The neighbor knew the girl liked dogs but never knew her back story —that she had wanted one for a while now.

Then the neighbor's dog gave birth to puppies. The little girl came by every day to see the them, until one day, the neighbor offered one to the little girl.

Her parents were at a loss of words because, even in their wildest dreams, they did not believe that a dog would come to their daughter through a channel such as this.

Now I really love this story, because this little girl has big things coming her way!

She's a magical force to be reckoned with.

There is a lot we can learn from this girl:

- She was clear about what she wanted.
- She made it known to the channels she believed could help her.
- She kept her mind on what she wanted.
- She never took it personal when she was refused a dog all that time—she was never desperate.
- She seized every opportunity she had to be closer to her desire. First by drawing it, then taking the collar, and finally, by appreciating the neighbor's dog.

That last point brings us to the fact that when you allow yourself to desire something, you must appreciate it wherever you see it.

If that little girl was an egocentric adult with the wrong ideas, it would have gone a whole lot differently.

She would have taken it personally when her parents said no, and she would have complained that they didn't love her enough to see what was important to her. That would have greatly hampered her ability to create the circumstances necessary for the ultimate achievement of her goal.

On the emotional line, wanting or desiring something is good, it is positive. Ideas and opportunities show up for you where you least expected them, and when you get what you want, everybody involved would have gained something—call it a win-win deal.

When you live on pure desire, something bigger than you, but residing in you, takes over. And that is where the ideas—or serendipity—would come through.

Desperation makes room for a win-lose situation. You may get what you want but you will lose something else. Desperation clouds thinking and because of that, it is very easy to make errors in a state of desperation.

Many of us don't allow ourselves to want things because we think it is too big to be accomplished, or that we don't deserve it. We were not born that way. We learned it from those who really didn't know how life works.

Try it out now. No matter where you are.

Think of something you really want. Not some whim or careless fancy. Think of something you really want. Imagine that you already have it.

Remember that the magnitude of your desire is inconsequential. Get into that imagination and really *feel* it. See it clearly. Surely you feel energized after this.

Let go of any thoughts that suggest it is too big or that you do not deserve it.

Focus on having it and believe in that image in your mind.

The more often you do this, the more you focus on your desires and really feel that you already have achieved it, the more serendipitous events will happen to bring that desire into your reality.

What begins to happen is that strange conversations and chances will start to occur in the direction of your desire. You will notice things you didn't notice before. What was background noise will become foreground and you will know that something is working in your favor—it is working because you set it in motion.

So, you see desire to have is fueled by the love. It is okay to want things, to desire things.

Some people don't even have TIME to spend with their loved ones. Such a person could genuinely desire to have time and focus on getting more.

Desire is not a flimsy whim based on the ego.

A bad example of desire would be:

"I want to get married because all my friends are getting married."

That desire is based on comparison and it does not end well for anybody.

A good example would be:

"I want to get married so I can enjoy the fulling relationship and companionship that comes with marriage."

The second example is based on an inward feeling seeking expression... It is based on the natural law of growth, and it will manifest for us because of that.

In a later chapter, we will discuss how desire is closely linked with letting go—which is another step to truly mastering your mindset and unleashing your inner magic.

Have you ever noticed that some people have a glow about them while others have a gloom?

Ever noticed some people are 'lucky' and others are 'unlucky'?

Have you ever thought that there must be some way to fix your life? To become magnificently rich? To buy that yacht you've always dreamed of?

Know this, my friend: it's possible. You have the power within yourself. Whether you have spent your life in a series of unfortunate events, or you've spent it in the lap of luxury, your mindset is what puts you there. And it's also what keeps you there.

'Luck' is totally within our control. However, we must know how to use what we have (our emotions) to get what we desire.

Imagine a ship. A giant ship on water, moving with such grace, capable of holding hundreds, maybe thousands of people with enough food and water to sustain them for months.

Now, this piece of machinery is an incredible invention, and the skill needed to be able to control the movement of this machine would not come easy. By turning a single wheel one can move this massive ship around and get it to do their bidding. A man with the proper knowledge and training can use this machine to travel the world, see every port, adventure to his content.

However, with poor control of this machine, misfortune and death is certain.

This machine is what we call 'luck'. Of course, we don't know exactly what tomorrow will bring. We don't know if we will absolutely get that job we wanted or if we will end up getting hit by a bus.

What we do have control over is how we react to things today. Our opinions we hold today, the judgments we hold today. These things shape our future.

Life Story:

Sandra is a lady who gets scared often. She grew up with her mother who was always worried, living life paycheck to paycheck, afraid of how they were going to "make it through the month."

Sandra has this terrible fear of being robbed, every time she hears a sound she jumps. She doesn't remember how it began, yet she constantly has this fear at the back of her mind.

For some reason, when she started living alone, she found that every house she lived in would always get broken into. Even if an area was normally very safe, when Sandra moved to that neighborhood, they start experiencing break ins and robberies.

Could Sandra's fear really be so powerful in order to cause these changes in her experience of life? Quite frankly, yes.

Whether we use our minds to focus on things that we desire to have which are positive, or whether we constantly worry and obsess over things which are negative, we will draw them into our lives.

Fear is insidious. Worry and stress are like a disease that creeps into our subconscious and can grow huge if left unchecked. We have to take it upon ourselves to start focusing on the good we want in life, and steering our thoughts away from the bad. If you practice this daily then you will begin to see how often your mind wants to worry you. And the more you practice it, the more you'll be able to flex the muscles of your subconscious mind to be positive thinking first.

Practice Your Power Exercise:

Write down a list of what you desire in life. This can contain anything from material things to career or relationship goals, and everything in between.

Now write down a list of negative thoughts that you have which relate to those desires. What are you scared of or projecting onto your desires that could be stopping you from achieving them?

Now turn that negative thought into a positive one! Do this for every desire that you have written down, and continue to re-asses this list as you keep pushing for your goals.

"The starting point of all achievement is Desire."
-Napoleon Hill

STEP FOUR

ACTIVE THOUGHT

"What we know is drop, what we don't know is the ocean."
-Isaac Newton

So far, we have accepted our past and who we are, we have discovered how to truly know what things are, we have allowed ourselves to desire what we desire, and we are instilling the belief inside ourselves that we can get it.

However, right now it is still in our head.

How do we stay focused on our new mindset?

How do we make sure that the naysayers out there don't dull our inner magic?

ACTIVE THOUGHT is the answer to that.

Active thought it simply the mindful way of thinking actively in the present and on positive emotions. Turning a negative thought into something positive the first time may not be so easy. But the more you think about something, the easier it becomes.

Remember my story about my dad getting me to smile when I was sad? At first it may be a bit difficult, but by thinking actively we can build the focus to persevere in our positivity.

We want to live positively, but we find ourselves thinking upbeat one minute and unfocused the next. It's a constant struggle between wanting to be positive, yet having negative thoughts intrude on us. This is normal for everyone. The goal is to let positivity win.

All thoughts create an impression, and they influence our emotions in the same direction. In turn, these emotions fuel the thought which originated them, making the thought stronger. Which in turn makes it easier to focus on that thought, because of the emotion associated with it.

When this emotion and thought are strong enough, we live in the spirit of our thought and we act as though that thought is already reality in the physical world. This makes thinking the thought and feeling the feeling easier every single time, till we cannot help but live in that thought and feeling every minute of every day.

Active thought can also be called conscious focus. The idea behind it is that when you think something consciously for a while, you can pass it to subconscious thought so you free up your consciousness to focus on other stuff.

An example is when riding a bicycle. At first you must think every action through. You have to make sure you are sitting right, then you ensure that the right leg moves first, and you have to know exactly when to lift the second leg from the floor. You then must remember the exact location of the pedals so you don't miss—it can be a lot of work.

But what happens when you have practiced for a little amount of time? It becomes second nature. You can do all of it without thinking about it.

It is the same with mastering your mindset. Due to the errors we learned in the past, we have to remind ourselves to be positive and to stay positive.

It's a matter of training our minds to replace a negative thought with a positive thought. It could be a lot of work at first, depending on how much errors we have to unlearn, but gradually we begin to get used to it.

We begin to imbibe it into our nature and before long, it is part of us. We will no longer struggle to stay positive.

Life Story:

Take Margaret, a single mom living in Manhattan, New York. She used to be very unhappy, she felt her lot in life was the worst, and she complained about everything and everyone. She was bitter day in and day out. It took a toll on her physical self, as well as on her emotions and her job, which she could barely keep.

Everything revolved around the facts that she focused on in her life, that she was:

Single.

A woman.

A single mother.

One couldn't even look at her without her lashing out with words like, "Oh! You've never seen a single mother before? You must think I am a stupid woman to have a child and be unmarried."

She felt segregated, she was constantly angry because of how she viewed herself. She felt lost and frustrated and alone. She also spent a lot of her time watching reality shows and news broadcasts filled with negativity.

Margaret became very hostile because of her thought patterns. She thought everyone was judging her, and that everyone was against her.

After a while, she realized—fortunately for her—that she was going to lose everything worth anything in her world.

This realization came when she was reported to child services. The report was that her erratic and hostile behavior made for an unsafe environment for her daughter, who was 6 years old at the time.

She didn't want her daughter taken from her, so she sought help.

She needed to be more positive for her daughter's sake—even if for nothing else.

Part of her treatment came in the form of active thought.

She was asked to repeat certain sentences:

There are many single mothers.

Being single is healthy and fine.

I am a part of my community.

I am a strong and independent.

I have a lot of love in my life.

I welcome more love into my life.

This was very difficult because all her life she had believed the opposite of this. How can you say there is nothing wrong?

Her mind could not—at first—accept this. She couldn't stand trying to actively think that nothing was wrong when things were definitely going wrong in her life. It was hard for her to switch gears and stop dwelling on the negative.

She was advised to listen to classical melodies like Beethoven, Handel, and Bach, as well as relaxing mediation music, to help her calm her mind. She took anger management classes and began to invest in her mind as she never had before.

She was asked to stop watching the shows she was used to having on in the background at home, and she started reading self-help books and watching positive shows instead.

Gradually she began to come around. She would lash out but not as often as before. She noticed that all the people who used to annoy her were reducing in number, not because they weren't there physically, but because now their comments didn't get to her as much as they used to.

She was more comfortable in her own skin and she could tolerate people more. She stopped being so reactive, and paused to think before she acted. She persevered through her change in both her outlook on others, and her outlook on herself. Today she is remarried and doing well in her job.

This is by no means easy at first but we can all push through.

Thomas Edison did.

Michael Faraday did.

William Shakespeare did.

Bill Gates did.

Tony Robbins did.

If they can do this with great success, then it is something we are all capable of. We can all do these things if we are willing to expend the effort necessary to accomplish such feats.

We started by dedicating this book to those who wished to rise above mediocrity. The methods outlined here will help you do that and more.

However, it is up to you to begin initiating these practices into your day to day life. Once you begin, you will find that it comes more naturally over time to face challenges and meet them with a positive mindset.

Practice Your Power Exercise:

To get begin practicing active thought, your mind must be quiet. You cannot think of a million things at once.

What you are to do now is activate a thought, and hold it in your mind, excluding other thoughts which will constantly be trying to pull focus.

Do this successfully for five minutes.

Then try for ten minutes.

Once you get a hang of this, you can begin switching gears in your daily life and actively stopping negative thoughts in their tracks.

STEP FIVE

GRATITUDE

Gratitude is a feeling.

What does it mean to be grateful?

Simply put: Gratitude means being thankful for something.

Yet gratitude is not words. It can be expressed as such, but gratitude is not simply words.

It is not simply saying thank you for something, it is the feeling that comes with that expression of gratitude.

Imagine this. You are on a road trip and your car breaks down at a point where there is no mechanic to fix it. Your phone has run out of charge and you can't reach anyone. Two hours go by and you are trying to flag down other road users, but it is a highway, no one is stopping.

Two more hours go by and it is getting dark, then you realize the darkness is not nighttime, it is a cloudy sky preparing to rain… The rain begins and you get into your car to wait it out, but the rain is not stopping. It pours and pours and synchronizes with the actual night that has come upon you.

Just when you have decided to spend the cold night in the car, you hear a knock on your window, and you find out the person is actually offering you help.

How does that feel? This stranger just saved you. At that time, you feel like you owe them everything.

That is what gratitude feels like.

Whatever you say at that point—be it thank you or anything else—is now an expression of that feeling of gratitude.

Gratitude is the surest way to bring more into our lives. I'm sure you are aware of the bestselling book 'The Secret' where Rhonda Byrne expertly explains the power of gratitude.

In 'The Secret' she explains that whatever we are grateful for, we get more of. If we are grateful for a dollar, we get more dollars; if we are grateful for clear skies, we get more clear skies.

We need to be grateful in every situation and for everything. Not just when things go well, but when they are not so perfect.

Being grateful for the good things is the easy part. But remember to be grateful for the little things, and to put a grateful, positive spin on the bad things too. For example, if you get to work five minutes late, be grateful that it wasn't thirty minutes late. If you get a stain on your favorite shirt just before you leave the house, be grateful it didn't happen when you couldn't change your outfit.

Gratitude shifts your energy from focusing on the negative to focusing on the good and the positive. And focusing on the good today will bring about good tomorrow. It is as simple as that.

That's the simple, yet incredible power of the magic within you.

You can choose to take it up a notch and be grateful for something that isn't even there yet. What would happen is that you create an even more tangible expectancy for what is to come.

Life Story:

Take Jonathan, an entrepreneur who owned a company that had been in the importation business for 5 years. His business was going well, and he never owed any debts. At least until one fateful day when two of his containers sank on the high sea, and he incurred debts that were so massive, they were greater than he could resolve without declaring bankruptcy.

He tried his best but a lot of investment had gone into this purchase and he was stranded. He remained positive, waking up knowing his business couldn't fail because of this, even though he faced negativity from other affected.

His bank was not happy as he had been loaned some money to assist in this investment, his clients who had expected goods were equally unhappy as they had made plans around the arrival of these goods.

He assured them to remain calm and that all would be fixed. He didn't know exactly how he was going to fix... he simply remained positive.

What he would do was ask himself "What do I want?" And the answer was simple. "I want my business to survive this period and come out stronger." He didn't know how to go about it, but Johnathan chose to keep on thinking and believing in what he wanted. He saw his vision of a successful, booming business and he never let that vision fade away.

With this mindset, he treated every new client with incredible respect and passion, because in his mind, any of these people could be is way out of the challenges he was facing.

He would often say, "I am grateful for the new clients I have coming in. There is always money coming into my business, money flows freely into my life."

He kept at this for months with no seeming change in his situation... but he stayed positive. When he would receive a call from an angry client, (perhaps filled with insults) of course, it would get to him at times. But he didn't wallow in the misfortune.

Just as soon as he got the calls, he shook them off, repeating firmly his mantra, "Money is flowing freely into my life." and "I am grateful for the success of my company."

One day a new client walked in off the street and said she was passing by and saw his firm. The client was a lady from New Zealand. She was an incredibly wealthy woman and looking to invest a massive amount of money. They had a meeting and the rest was history. She felt comfortable with his business, he explained to her his misfortune and how he was working on fixing it. His business was saved.

Here we see that it all works together in mastering your mindset to overcome obstacles.

To practice gratitude, get out a piece of paper and a pen, write down all that you are grateful for.

Start small, write twenty today, then write thirty the next time.

You should express your gratitude for everything, no matter how seemingly insignificant it may be. When people tell me their lives are miserable, and that they have nothing to be grateful for, I always tell them to check their pulse. Start with that.

When I do this exercise, I start off with obvious things. Things that easily come to my mind, like my family, my job, my life. And then begins a kind of grateful torrent of people, places and things that I am grateful for.

I begin to feel almost high from the emotions that I am able to find within myself when expressing gratitude for my life and all that is in it.

If you struggle at first to find things to be grateful for, start out small. Be thankful for your hands, your eyes, your sight. Be grateful for the chair you're sitting on as you write the list. For the roof over your head, and the food in your belly.

There is much and more to be grateful for. You will see. Just begin.

Rhonda Byrne, best-selling author of 'The Secret', tells of the power of gratitude in a story of gratitude: How a man had a rock which remained in his pocket.

I love this story so I want to share it with you again here.

Whenever he touched this rock, he would think of the things he was grateful for.

One day a colleague saw it with him and asked what it was for. After the man explained the reason that he kept the stone, his colleague started to call it a 'gratitude rock'.

Time passed and some months later, he got an email from the colleague which said that his son was diagnosed with a certain kind of hepatitis and there was no cure in sight.

He asked this man to send him 'gratitude rocks' and he would begin a practice in the art of gratitude. He had been told that gratitude shifts energy and he believed in the power of gratitude to repel the sickness.

This was just a stone this man found but he gave it a shot. He went to a nearby stream and picked some fine stones which he mailed to the man with the sick son.

About a month after the rocks were received, the news was a good one. The man's child was recovered, and they made a business of selling 'gratitude rocks' and raising money for charity.

You don't have to wait until you have the things you want in life to begin to be grateful for them, start now to be grateful for any and everything.

Here are some examples of gratitude:

- I am grateful for my family.
- I am grateful for my body.
- I am grateful that both my hands still work and that I can hold this book.

- I am grateful for each breath I take that keeps me alive and strong.
- I am grateful that I have a roof over my head.
- I am grateful for my eyes, and the ability to see the world each day.
- I am grateful that I am always on time for my appointments.
- I am grateful that my brain works, and that I can be coordinated.
- I am grateful that I leave my house every day and come back safely.
- I am grateful that I can pay my own bills.
- I am grateful that I have people who love me for who I am.

The little things you think don't matter, do matter immensely. Find them and appreciate them.

Appreciate that friend who is always in control of his emotions, appreciate that lady who is always punctual.

Appreciate the bad situations too, because they make you stronger and better. Something bad has happened to everyone at some point in their life. For some, those bad things are debilitating, for others, they might not seem so terrible.

Never pass judgement on another for their situations and learn to appreciate the lessons you have learned from the tough places you've been in your life too.

Practicing gratitude like this moves your energy positively and makes for more good things in the future.

That is the magic you have inside you, that is true mastery of your mindset. You can move mountains with gratitude, so making it a daily practice to express gratuity in even the simplest of things and watch the magic flow into your life.

That is the truth.

Practice Your Power Exercise:

Find an object like the gratitude rock example share in this chapter and keep it in your possession. It doesn't have to be a rock. It could be a pen, a flower, your favorite handkerchief... you get the idea.

For myself I have a tiny metal stone that belonged to my older sister, Tamara. When she passed away, my mum gave it to me. It has the word 'love' engraved on it. Throughout the day, I list of the things I am grateful for out loud and I stroke the stone.

When I do this, I imagine the gratitude filling my heart and surrounding me like a warm golden blanket of positive energy. I visualize the love that comes with being grateful as a bright golden light coming from inside me and bursting out, coating everything in its warm glow. I imagine this light reaching out to envelope my friends and family, my loved ones.

The more often you practice this, the deeper it will instill in you the magic of gratitude. You will learn to be appreciative a lot more often.

Another exercise I practice nightly is writing a Gratefulness Journal. I highly recommend this as it ends the day with a feeling of eternal gratefulness and peace in your mind and heart. I keep a journal beside my bed, and every night I write down at least three things that happened throughout the day that I am grateful for.

Even on the worst of days, when you climb into bed and feel as though nothing went right for you, you will be able to find three things to be grateful for.

Perhaps the sun was shining, your dog or cat snuggled you when you got home, you had a good conversation with a loved one, someone complimented you...

It doesn't have to be a huge thing; it can be anything.

But as you do this practice more and more, you will begin to see that these seemingly minor things we write down are in fact huge things to be grateful for!

You are grateful for the roof over your head, you paid your bills on time, you had food for the day and didn't go hungry, you have clothes to wear, a place to sleep, your heart is beating.

By forcing yourself to think of three things that you're grateful for, you immediately project a serious dose of mindset mastery into your life, and you will find yourself becoming more and more grateful for everything in your life.

Focusing on the good things that you are grateful for creates a positive space and aura around your mindset.

This means that you will not have the time or energy to be looking at the negative things of life, or the things you do not like, or the things that are annoying.

"It is not happy people who are thankful.
It is thankful people who are happy."
-Anonymous

STEP SIX

AFFIRMATIONS

"I am strong, I am powerful, I am happy.
I have an endless flow of money coming into my life."
-Sarah Hall

Affirmations are messages (usually short messages) which we repeat to ourselves in order to keep our minds focused on a goal. We can think of these as our magical spells, the words we utter to bring about good in our lives. They are our mantras.

Every day you can cast a countless number of what could be called magical spells into the world around you, projecting your magic and visions into the universal energy, and therefore creating your very own dreams.

You can bring wonderful things into fruition.

You just need the vessel to accomplish those dreams, and lucky for you, that vessel is YOU.

We had a little preview of what these messages are in the previous chapter when we examined the story of Jonathan.

Affirmations work on the creative mind and for this purpose there are a few conditions necessary for them to work:

- An affirmation must be stated in the positive and present tense for best results.
- Affirmations must focus on the end result and not on the process of achieving the result.
- The best time to repeat your affirmation is just after you wake up and just before you go to sleep—the mind

is most receptive at those moments between sleep and wake state.

- An affirmation should focus on *being* and not on *having* —although both do work.

Life Story:

Ashton, a marketer from England, decided to test run affirmations just to see what he would get. It was back when iPhones were just released and they were the talk of the town. He wanted one. He admired the features and he knew having that phone would greatly improve his business.

This is what he wanted for his next phone, however at that point of his life, he could not afford one. And he was working his day job in the marketing department at Information Technology.

He decided to make up an affirmation in order to secure a phone.

He made up a short, positive, present statement concerning what he wanted:

"I am using an iPhone to improve to my business."

He repeated this to himself silently as soon as he woke up from sleep. Not just once. He repeated it till he forgot he was actually saying something in his mind.

He got to a point where he would start saying it without remembering he was saying it. He would just catch himself saying it.

He took it a step further and started buying iPhone news subscriptions from any of his friends who were using an iPhone at the time.

One day his manager called him to his office and said to him, "Ashton, do you have an iPhone? You are a marketer and I think it would help you in your duties."

Ashton was shocked to hear this.

He thought to himself:

"Could it really be that these affirmations are working?"

It didn't end there. The manager said the company was going to buy him one and within three days from that meeting, Ashton was officially an iPhone user, and the universe changed people, places and situations to get him what he desired without him having to buy it for himself.

Let us review those rules for creating positive affirmations. The affirmation must be short, positive, and in the present tense.

Bad example #1:

"I will be using an iPhone someday."

This statement is short and positive, but it is in the future—that does not work for us. When you use words like 'someday', 'one day' or 'soon', you are in fact delaying it from ever happening!

We need our affirmations to be in the present time.

A good example would be:

"I USE AN IPHONE."

Bad example #2:

"I am not poor."

Again short, but negative. That statement focuses on poverty.

A good affirmation would say:

"I AM WEALTHY."

The affirmation must focus on the end result.

Bad example #3:

"I am using a car I got from the Volvo dealership at a 50% off sale price."

This affirmation for getting a new car is not clear enough and has way too much restrictive detail. Volvo can't possibly be the only place to get a car, and a specific sale price is far too restrictive, and unless you specifically want a Volvo, do not include that make of car. Instead replace it with the exact car you want.

The Universe has lots of ways in which you will be supplied with our goal. It is not your place to put restrictive details on what you want.

The more you practice using and developing your own personal mantras, the better you will become at manifesting your desires.

A good example if you wanted to create an affirmation for a new car would be:

"I AM DRIVING A _____."

(List off the make, year, model, everything detailed down to the seats.)

An affirmation should focus on being, not having. This is because it is a law of life that you must be before you can have. So, focusing on having is focusing on the effect and not the cause. We can look at it from many angles and we would discover this truth.

A good mantra for bringing more money into your life is this:

"I love money, and money loves me."

Or:

"Money flows freely into my life, I have money coming in constantly, and bank account is full."

Or:

"I am grateful for money because (fill in the blank)."

Some other examples of thought patterns are these:

- Sandra HAS a husband. But Sandra had to BE a loving person in order to have a husband.
- Frank HAS a stroke. But you see, Frank has BEEN an unhealthy eater for many years.
- Ashton HAS an iPhone. But Ashton IS a dedicated marketer, so the phone came to him using that channel.

It is all around us. We must first be before we can have. So, focus on being the kind of person who drives a good car. That means you must look and talk and think a certain way.

You can't desire a new BMW while at the same time hating on those who are already driving new BMW's. You can't desire a brand-new car while not taking care of the one you already have.

As you use this skill more and more every day, you may realize that you are making affirmations (mostly negative!) without even realizing it.

We walk into a store and see an expensive piece of clothing that we like, and before we can stop ourselves, we mentally say something like, "I could never afford that" or, "Wow! That's ridiculously expensive." We have just affirmed to ourselves in our inner-most subconscious mind that we can't afford to buy this article of clothing, and that stops us from getting it today, but it also stops us from getting it next year, and the year after that. What we don't realize at the time is that we are dooming our chances of ever affording it.

Of course, you might think that it would be silly to look at the dress and say, "I can afford it!" when there is nothing in your bank account. I've been there! However, mastering your mindset to truly BELIEVE that you can afford it is better because when you say, "I can afford it!" you set yourself up to be ABLE to afford it in the future. And as I've mentioned before, the Universe has magical ways of bending the rules and giving you a way to buy that dress/car/house/boat/toothbrush that you've always wanted.

Remember we are always using our present to create our future. In a later chapter we are going to discuss what it means to live in the present and we will see how it relates to what we are discussing here.

So, focus on 'being' when you are affirming. Affirm, I AM CREATIVE, and you will become more creative daily.

Now, when I say that you want to affirm to be able to obtain, I am not talking purely material things. Not at all. I am talking more of the intangible things that money can't buy. For example, some intangible things that a creative person may have are:

- Talent in a certain field.
- The ability to make things from nothing.
- The ability to innovate.
- A sense of humor.

- To be in touch with his own thought.
- A lot of quiet time.

So, remember, the goal becomes focusing on being and not having, because once you are, having will flow automatically.

Practice Your Power Exercise:

Write down a list of affirmations that you will begin saying out loud daily. Write them down on post-it notes and stick them around your house everywhere, in places that you can see easily such as the fridge, the bathroom mirror, in your office, or even post them above your bed on the ceiling so when you lie down and look up you can fall asleep reading those affirmations over and over again.

Take it a step further and write them down as notifications that pop up on your phone, there are apps that let you do this and the app will send you a push notification with the affirmation on it periodically throughout the day. I've used the app 'YAP' in the past and it's great. You can also set yourself up daily alarms with your affirmations on them, or write them down and carrying them around in your wallet.

"It is the repetition of affirmations that lead to belief. And once that belief becomes a deep conviction, things begin to happen."
-Mohammed Ali

STEP SEVEN

IMAGINATION

"Imagination is the reality of the dreamer."
-Scott Ringenbach

I absolutely love this quote. It so describes my life that I feel as though I represent this notion in its entirety. That's how you should feel when you are truly passionate about something. Like it's a part of you, you live and breathe it.

I have always been a dreamer and a doer, when those two worlds collide with the law of attraction, pure magic begins to unleash itself into your life in tidal waves.

For me, there is nothing more fulfilling than imagining something and then bringing it to life. Like a story, a work of art, or a project that I've completed successfully.

It's like magic once I see it alive, when it was once only a thought in my head. An idea I had that I fed until it bloomed into its beautiful end product.

Like this book.

Whatever you see in this world was imagined before it could become physical. This makes cultivating the imagination one of the best skills we could develop and master.

To build a car, the engineers must first see it in their heads before it can become a physical reality. A house can never be started until the drawings and plans have been complete.

A book could not have been written had the author not imagined it first.

Think of your imagination as the drawings and plans from which your life will unfold.

Whatever it is you choose to accomplish, imagine it and it is guaranteed that eventually it will become real enough to be physical.

Life Story:

Maureen lived in a very poor setting most of her life; Her house was falling apart as it had been for as long as she remembered. There were leaks everywhere and the living conditions were not suitable.

Sure, she wanted to improve her living conditions but she did not have the finances with which to do that.

She searched for a way until she met a friend who told her about using the imagination to secure more positive living conditions.

This was strange to her because she believed that imagination was a waste of time for her, it was to be left to day dreamers and fiction writers. But her friend explained to her that imagination was not the same as daydreaming.

She began the exercises given to her by her friend just for the curiosity of it. The exercise involved Maureen thinking exactly how she wanted her house to look in her head, and then imagining as intensely as she could that she already had that house.

She was to be vivid and thorough in her imagination, and she was to keep at it till it manifested... no matter how long it took. She was to feel exactly how she would feel when she achieved her dream house, and when that picture was clear, she was to live in this wrecked house as though it was the dream house.

That meant that when she was about to boil water on the firewood place, she imagined and felt as though it was a gas-powered oven. She did not tell anyone what was going on in her head but she kept at it.

What this did to her is that she stopped feeling gloomy about the things she lacked in life, and instead, she smiled more and had this glow because she was in a world of her own. The physical challenges that were pitted against her became too small to stand up against her imagination... She had awoken a fire within.

What happened is that one day, as she was paying for her groceries at a local market, a man behind her in the line introduced himself as a casting director at an agency in town. He told her he was looking for a hand-model to advertise some creams for a cosmetic company whose portfolio he managed.

He gave her his card and said should she consider it, that she had very lovely hands and the spot was open provided she would come for a screening.

"A 'hand-model'? What in the world is that?" she asked her friend who was also hearing about it for the first time. So, she called, found that the pay was good, and Maureen took the job. Surely enough, after a few casting calls, Maureen's hand had been featured in several TV commercials, something she had never even considered before the opportunity had presented itself.

Maureen was making good money from each job and in 8 months she had restructured her house and felt her life changing for the better. Whenever she recounted the story to friends or family, she called it a true miracle... She explained that it was something within her, that she was responsible for the casting agent finding her and offering her the job.

Maureen explained to anyone who would listen that what had happened to make her life change for the better was that she aligned with an ability she never knew she had. And guess what? She ran with it.

Did it take consistency and perseverance?

YES!

Did it happen automatically?

NO!

Did it happen in a way that she thought would happen?

NOT IN HER WILDEST DREAMS!

But she pushed through and imagined her way out of that poor situation she found herself in.

Maureen didn't know how the money would come about, all she did was start to imagine a life where she had money coming in, and she really got into the feeling of that imagination, so much so that the present physical circumstances had no hold on her.

Daydreaming will destroy brain cells because there is no specific purpose or feeling attached to it.

It is random, uncontrolled images which are time consuming and unproductive.

Real imagination is visualization. It is holding an image of something that is yet to exist physically and making it real in your mind, with the purpose of getting it, or creating it, and the full assurance that you can have it… That it already is.

You eventually get to the point where you can imagine anything. All it takes is time, but you become unstoppable.

You start small as with everything else, and decide that you will succeed before you stop.

Once you decide that you will succeed—no matter what it is, no matter how—then you will be able to achieve what you may have once looked upon as impossible. Nothing is truly impossible.

Remember, if one person can do it, have it or be it, then ANY person can do it, have it, or be it. Regardless of their status or background, their wealth (or lack thereof), or where they grew up, ANY person can do it, have it or be it. Anyone. And that anyone can be YOU. There is endless money, talent and knowledge in this Universe.

Whatever you desire your life to be like, the Universe wants you to have it. You just have to let it in by mastering your mindset to create abundance and unleash your inner magic.

This is why you should succeed, if you let yourself fail, then you doom yourself to another failure in the future, and with every failure in this endeavor, the chances of success reduce.

Laziness will cost us everything, should we choose to indulge it. We need to rise above and imagine a greater, more fulfilling life, so that we can use our inner magic to make it real.

To use your imagination requires nothing from you in terms of physical strength, it is a skill anyone and everyone can develop and it is readily available, because you already have it inside yourself, even if you don't exercise it now.

It's there and it's waiting for you to awaken it. Deep down you know that all you need to succeed is your will power, and a little push from yourself to start. Then you have to keep pushing, every single day, keep moving towards your goals without fear.

Remember this:

You need to fight for what you want NOW, or else you will end up fighting against what you don't want later.

Practice Your Power Exercise:

What is it that you imagine your life could be like? What are your biggest dreams? Write them all down. Don't hold back or limit yourself. People have a bad tenancy to prevent themselves from dreaming big because they fear that if they dream too big then people might judge them.

Don't stop yourself from writing down the biggest dreams you have.

If you want to travel to Outerspace, write it down!

The next step is using a vision board to create the visualization required on a larger scale. You can make a vision board for your house by cutting out photos from magazines of things that are very specific to your goals and pinning them to a corkboard, or gluing them on some poster board. You can also write things down, or print photos off the internet.

When I wanted to move to the UK, I hung a UK flag up on my vision board. You can create a vision board for many things, including, but not limited to, a relationship you want to have, a job you want to get, a certain income you want to be earning, places you want to travel to and even health goals you want to achieve.

Put the vision board somewhere you will see it every single day. Spend some time every day looking at the photos and words you've written down, imagining what your life will look like once it's achieved, really FEEL how it feels to have the wind blowing through your hair as you're tanning on your brand new super yacht, or how the love between you and your future husband feels. Then trust that the universe will start drawing these into your life.

> *"Much gathers more. Loss leads to greater loss."*
> *–Charles Haanel*

STEP EIGHT

PATIENCE

"Bread must rise, and cake must bake, things must take the time they take."
-Walt Disney

If I left this chapter with only that quote from one of the most creative and imaginative people of this century, then surely you would be able to take an important lesson from that quote alone.

Patience is a virtue that carries a lot of 'wait' (get it?). It cannot be over-emphasized. To be patient means that you are well aware of your rights, and that you know that nothing and no one can take what is rightfully yours.

To be patient means that you are fully aware that there is no such thing as 'too late'.

To be patient means you have put aside feelings like desperation and fear.

To be patient means to have a calm mind.

And to be patient, you must be tested.

Think about this:

How do you know you are strong if there is nothing to test that strength?

How do you know you are fast if there is no avenue in which to test that speed?

And like every other test, it isn't easy.

Life Story:

A poor farmer sought to improve the conditions of his family. He heard that bamboo was soon becoming a major export for his country and that bamboo farmers would be the next millionaires, so he decided to start bamboo farming.

He secured a piece of property for a small amount of money. The land was cheap because there was no water in those areas.

It was a hill, and even when it rained, water rarely got into the land as it would roll downhill to the valley. Still it was a good buy in his opinion and he went for it.

The only thing is that he would have to go uphill every day to water whatever he planted. But he thought it would be worth it in the end, He thought once his bamboo is harvested in a couple of months, he would be rich.

His friend who told him of this opportunity was a traveler and he heard of it from a neighboring city. This farmer had never planted bamboo and he had no idea what it took to harvest such a plant.

However, he got all he needed and he planted.

The water he hauled and the distance to the land was quite tiring. The land was on the outskirts so he had to carry water from his residence, climb up the hill with it, and return.

He did the same every day.

Six months passed and there was still no evidence that he had planted something.

One year passed, and at this point he began to wonder if he had planted it right, a thought occurred to him—uproot and confirm that it was well sowed.

Yet the farmer couldn't do that because that would mean killing off the plants he'd been so patiently waiting to bloom.

Six more months passed and by now he was already a laughing stock. He said he had gone this far and he didn't see why he should stop.

Yes, he was discouraged, but what would he gain if he stopped now? The people of the town were already laughing at him so he had no ego to protect... so he continued. Every day hauling up water with no apparent result. It was so easy for him to give up but he did not... He continued patiently.

The victory came about three years after he planted the seedlings. He went up to water it one morning and he saw a small shoot. He was overjoyed and, of course, he remained zealous in watering his plant.

What he learned about the bamboo tree is that it takes only weeks to get to full maturity after it has germinated, but it takes 3 long years to get to that stage. Within a month, he was making contact and talking to investors who were willing to do business with him. He started exporting his bamboo and his family never lacked again.

It is easy to lose hope and patience especially when we don't know exactly how much time it will take for our desires to manifest.

But as J.K Rowling once said through the wise words of Professor Dumbledore,

"There comes a time where we must choose between what is right, and what is easy."

You can practice meditation as a way to begin introducing patience into your life. When I was growing up, and even to this day, patience hasn't been my best quality. So, I meditate, and keep practicing, and I will probably continue for life because the way my mental focus and clarity is when I meditate is amazing!

It takes focus to learn patience, and understanding within yourself.

I suffered through anxiety and worry for most of my teenage and early adult life, and you won't believe how many times people told me to try mediating. I thought I couldn't do it (another mental mindset block!), and therefore I never bothered to even try. And so, I just kept on continuously suffering through anxiety and stress and senseless worrying.

Finally, as I grew older, wiser and really began expanding my consciousness through hitting up the spirit gym, I learned to adjust my own mindset about meditation.

Turns out it's pretty easy. Essentially you just breathe with your eyes shut, and when a new worry or thought pops into your head, you simply thank it for attending, and dismiss it. Then keep on breathing.

If you're stubborn (as I was), and stuck in the "I can't do this" mentality, be patient!

You have to accept that it may not be easy to learn patience, but it's worth the wait.

When you feel stuck or confined, a calm mind will let you see the situation for what it really is, and it will be easier to find solutions.

Our brains work on the fight or flight survival instinct, and if we are unable to maintain a calm mind to find a solution to the problem, then the brain will go into overdrive, hence anxiety and worrying.

Patience requires that you understand that time is merely an illusion. It is not as real as we think it is. Ever notice how time moves faster when you are doing something enjoyable, and how it seems to slow down when your activities are minimal?

Have you seen that when you are traveling, the distance of the return trip is usually shorter than it was when you were going on the trip?

This really shows us that time is what we make of it, our perception of time is completely relative.

That is another part of the magic we have within us, the ability to control time itself.

We create our own reality.

Sounds a bit hocus-pocus?

Maybe it does, but the truth of the matter is that we are able to live full and meaningful lives with everything we desire… or we can dwell on the past and make our own lives miserable.

When we have grasped the fact that we can create our own realties, we will begin to understand the need to allow things to take the required time to manifest. Now don't get me wrong here, you cannot change those bad things that have happened to you in your life. Unfortunately, no one can. But how we chose to move forwards and move on with our lives is what really matters.

Everything in life needs time to get from one place to another. Plants need time to grow, a pregnancy needs nine months to birth. And so, it goes.

When was the last time you were impatient? Do you remember what caused it? Perhaps you felt there wasn't enough time? What triggered it?

Some people find themselves impatient when they are stuck in traffic, others when they have to wait what feels like ages for their wives to finish applying make-up. Maybe you find that you're impatient to get through the day at work, or impatient waiting in line at the bank.

Now imagine if you just lived in the present moment and appreciated where you were. Whether it's waiting in line or stuck in traffic, imagine that you just could just BE PRESENT without you losing your nerve. Without being impatient and getting frustrated with having to wait.

Impatience causes one to tense up and make poor decisions. It can cause anger, stress and fighting. We end up realizing that our impatience was not really necessary in the first place! What's the point in becoming aggravated over something as silly as waiting in a line? No point!

Whenever you find yourself getting heavy with impatience, it would do you well to remember the following points:

- There is more than enough time.
- Time is an illusion.
- Impatience distorts judgment.

And I say, why not choose patience? From here on out, I want you to focus on being positive, and with patience comes a lot of positivity.

Life Story:

Kylie works as a teller in the bank. She sees hundreds of people in a day, and once in a while they could have a crowd, which creates longer wait times for customers.

Every single time they get backed up, there are always those people who cannot wait for one reason or another. They soon become enraged and begin shouting or treating her poorly because they have somewhere else to be.

When she would ask them to be a little patient, they would sometimes respond saying, "I have been patient enough!" But you see therein lays the error in our thinking.

Patience has no expiry. To be patient means to wait until whatever you are waiting for is ready for *you*. Being patient does not mean to wait until you are tired of waiting! And you most certainly won't achieve a happy life by treating others poorly due to your OWN lack of patience.

So next time you feel yourself becoming impatient, repeat this mantra:

I have more than enough time.

The more you think that you're going to be late when you're driving to work in rush hour traffic, the more likely you are to be late.

Yet when you stop yourself from projecting stress and negative energy into the Universe—simply by repeating that there's more than enough time—you are projecting positivity and the Universe will find a way for you to arrive on time.

Practice Your Power Exercise:

The Simplest Meditation Ever.

Seriously.

If I can do this, you can – I promise.

1. Sit in a comfortable chair with your back straight.
2. Close your eyes and try to keep your mind blank.
3. Place both your palms on your thighs.
4. Take a deep breath in.

5. Breathe out.
6. Focus on keeping your mind clear. If thoughts creep in, acknowledge them, then release them and continue breathing.
7. Repeat the process and take note on how the muscles of your body start to relax. First your shoulders, then your arms, then your back and your waist muscles, then feel your legs and toes also relax.

This exercise is very important if we are to learn the art of patience. So, don't just do it once and give up. Do it daily. The only person that you'll be letting down if you don't practice your powers is yourself. Don't forget it.

"Patience is not the ability to wait; it is the attitude we display while waiting."
-Joyce Meyer

STEP NINE

LETTING GO

"You only lose what you cling to."
-Buddha

Just how much do you think you can control in this world? The answer is that you can control everything… and at the same time, you control nothing.

Let me explain.

In your inner world, you are in total control. The inner world controls the outer world, so, in a way, you can also control the outer world. This means that, yes, you control everything.

But very few people know about the world of subconscious thoughts and feelings, so they try to control outward events. They try to control people and the world around them.

These people who try to control everything soon get exhausted and bitter because, let's face it, if you are not in control of your thoughts, feelings and actions, then you control nothing.

Can you see what I mean when I say you control everything and nothing at the same time?

If you have spent time cultivating patience through positive affirmations or meditation and breathing exercises, if you've begun a journey to knowing yourself and being comfortable in your own skin, if you have forgiven the past and used your imagination to visualize your future: you'll find that you don't have to control people—or any outward event for that matter.

That is where letting go comes in.

Letting go is when you allow yourself to feel that you have done what you should do in any given situation, and then believe that you have done all that you can do.

You are to let the outward world align to what you have built in your inner mindset, and that is the true reward of mastering your mindset and drawing positive energy into your life.

You don't have to *force* anything to bow to you and do your bidding. It is not necessary to shout and scream at people. If someone doesn't want to do what you've asked of them, is shouting and screaming at them really going to help? Really? No, sorry, it's not.

Your only job should be to build positivity in your mindset by carefully choosing thoughts and feelings that empower you.

The true practice of letting go might look like indifference to others, but what they don't understand is that by letting go, you have projected to the Universe the action of making your inner world beautiful.

When you let go, you no longer have a problem with decision-making. You know that whatever you decide is going to be the best thing for you.

Tell me that this isn't positive enough to keep you smiling and happy indefinitely.

There is an inner peace that comes with the ability to let go. It allows us to explore life in all its ramifications, and we end up living more when we cease to attempt to control outward events. Things are not created outwardly, so, trying to control and change them from the outside is a complete and utter waste of time.

For example, if you print out a document and find an error on the copy, it's ok to wipe out that error with a correcting fluid. What isn't ok is printing another copy and getting upset that the error is persisting. We do not want to be that person. We should practice letting go every day when we find ourselves trying to change external events (or people) because they make us feel negative.

We should be reminded that that:

- Nobody owns us.
- We don't own anybody.
- We should never infringe on another person's rights.
- No one has the right to infringe on our rights.

In many parts of the world we face a challenge where parents want to live their children's lives for them. They feel that because they are parents, they have every right above their child. But in reality this is simply not supposed to be the way.

The job of a parent is to guide and lead by example. You cannot tell your child what to study in school, you cannot tell them what industry to work in, and you cannot tell them who to marry.

If we, as parents, have done our job of offering guidance and leading by example, then we should be confident in our child's decisions regarding their life, and not try to infringe upon it.

Many parents failed in their own lives and didn't end up achieving their dreams. They didn't marry the person they wanted, they didn't go to the school they would have liked to and they didn't pursue the career they loved. Because of this they feel on a subconscious level that their child would follow the same path of failure. It is because of this we hear of parents dictating a child's life from inception to career and eventually marriage.

It is true that a person's decision-making part of their brain does not fully develop until about age 25. So yes, at any point prior to that age, the child may not actually know what he wants. Or perhaps he thinks he knows what he wants, or what is best for him, but actually does not.

It is then the job of the parent to hear the child's point of view, and listen with understanding so as to better explain the reason for his own parental decisions—not out of a need to control their child, but out of love and guidance and interest in that child's future and welfare.

Have you ever noticed that the children who grow up in the more 'restrictive' environments grow up to be the wilder and looser ones?

Meanwhile, the ones who were allowed a fair amount of freedom turn out more responsible and coordinated?

Now while that certainly isn't always the case, there is a good example I can share of cultures which show this fairly well. In Italy, kids are allowed to have a small glass of wine with dinner on occasion, and they grow up thinking that alcohol is something to be enjoyed with dinner in small amounts and not abused. In North America, kids are never allowed even a sip of alcohol and are told how bad it is for them. As such, when they become teenagers, often times they will seek out ways to sneak alcohol and abuse it, because they didn't grow up thinking nothing of it.

If we come across a negative situation and we feel like we must act on it from the outside, first take a deep breath, think about it, and then if you must say something, make it constructive and calm, then walk away. Stay calm and relaxed and everything externally will follow suit.

A big part of letting go is also about letting go of bad situations and people in your life that may be using up your energy.

A good way to recognize if a certain person or situation needs to be let go is by stopping and taking a moment to see how you feel when you are with them.

Weigh the relationship you have with them on your inner dial.

Is it a heavy feeling you get?

Or is it a light and easy feeling you get?

Do you feel care free and happy?

Or does spending time with that person make you feel drained and tired, worn out and lethargic?

If it's any of the latter, then they are quite literally sucking the magic out of you and you need to consider spending less time with them or in those situations.

There are some people who, regrettably, may always be a toxic energy, and for the sake of our wellbeing, we need to distance ourselves from them.

The more that you focus your energy on self-improvement, the more you will notice the negative, draining people you may have in your life. You also may notice that YOU were in fact the negative draining person! But don't fear because guess what? You're working on it! Just reading this book is a giant step towards a healthy change in your life.

There are also others who may not realize the impact they are having on you—or themselves, for that matter. Try talking with someone you care about who is causing you toxicity in your life and see if they are willing to, or have the desire for change before you have to let go of their negative energy altogether.

You may also have trauma that has happened years ago, which you may have buried down and tried to forget about. Or perhaps there is fresh trauma that you've recently gone through that you need to give yourself space to heal from before letting go of it. Sometimes you will not be able to gain closure from a painful experience that happened to you, or you may not be able to forgive that person for what they did to you. The important thing here is to forgive yourself, to love yourself and to allow yourself to heal.

If someone has hurt you, I want you to remember that many people hurt others because they have pain inside them. So, wishing them pain for hurting you isn't going to bring you any closer to healing. As hard as it can be to wish healing on someone who hurt you, it may help to understand and acknowledge that the person who caused you pain is not happy within their own heart. Hurt people hurt people.

There is no sense in hurting others to try to 'get even'. Remove them from your life. Grieve the situation. Work on yourself and giving yourself all the love you have to give. Then let go and move on.

Practice Your Power Exercise:

Write a list of things that you know in your heart you need to let go of. Things that are causing you pain, bringing toxicity and negativity into your life. Things that are traumatic that you either haven't forgiven someone for, or haven't forgiven yourself for. Write everything down.

No one will see this list. In fact, after you're done – burn it.

In the act of letting go we begin to make room for more positive people and situations to come flowing into our lives.

Let it all go.

Author's Note

There may be some traumatic experiences which you need counselling or treatment from a doctor for. Please do actively seek medical attention for trauma and any kind of triggering emotions that come up. It's healthy to seek expert help when needed. I have been in counselling for over a decade on and off, and it's changed my life. There are somethings I went through, such as sexual, physical and emotional abuse which caused PTSD and anxiety disorders that I needed professional help with. Never be afraid to ask for help or to share your story in a safe environment with someone you trust.

"Letting go does not mean that you stop caring; it means you stop forcing others to."
-Anonymous

STEP TEN

LIVING IN THE MOMENT

"You must live in the present... find your eternity in every moment."
-Henry Thoreau

What does it mean to live in the moment? Many of us do not know. Many of us have lived so much of our lives in a kind of constant mental turmoil.

However, I bet we do know what it feels like to not know what is happening around us. We no longer pay attention to the people and scenarios around us.

So many of us are stuck in a strange kind of limbo, caught between thinking about what is to come or what has already been, that we forget what *is*.

We get into a car, get to our destination, do what we have to do, get back outside and head home. If you were asked what was the first thing you saw when you stepped into that building, you may quickly realize that you do not remember.

We are always in a hurry to some future event or trying to fix the past. We misplace things because we don't pay attention. One second our keys are in our hands and the next second we have misplaced them, not remembering where we dropped them.

One minute we are using our cell phones, the next minute we are having a mental breakdown because we cannot find it! (Although it's sitting on our desk. Am I right?)

Simply put, we are absent minded. Why?

Why are we a culture of absent-minded people? It's because we are always living in and expecting the future, which hasn't been written yet... Or we are living in the past.

We forget to take note of the rainbow in the sky, the chirping of the birds, the whistling of the wind, the wonders that surround us. We forget to have a conversation with the person alone in the elevator with us, and instead stare blankly at our cell phone, even though it doesn't get reception in there.

Life Story:

James was a successful business man. His life and career took off and before he knew it, he was living in his own house, married and expecting a child. With more success came more business and more work. His hours at the office increased and his hours at home rapidly reduced.

He barely knew his wife anymore, and despite the fact he was bringing home more money, he simply was not around. On the day of his son's birth he was in Japan taking care of business.

He thought he was out making for a better life for his family, so that his son could have the life he never had.

But in doing so, he continued to lose himself. When his son turned five James realized that he had never been with the boy on his birthday to celebrate.

He knew deep down his family was slipping away from him, all because he did not live in the moment with them. Even in the rare times he was at home, James was always on the phone, texting or answering emails.

Within five minutes of holding a conversation with his wife, he would receive a call and then that would last thirty minutes. He forgot anniversaries, dinners, movie trips. He didn't have time to take his family on vacations.

He lived his whole life like this. Eventually, his wife divorced him because she felt constantly unloved. His son grew up and married, distancing himself from his already distant father. He rarely visited his grandchildren, and when he did, they were shy around him and didn't know him.

When James was on his death bed, the one thing he regretted more than anything was not being present in his life with his family. He realized in the final years of his life that he had missed out on what life really was – family, love and happiness.

Hearing this, I hope you think that you don't ever want to be like James. But at the same time, maybe you don't realize that in some ways you already are.

Consider the fact that we are often found either soaked in the past, or feeling anxious about the future. We are not present. We are not here where we need to be.

This is a very simple task, just like everything we have discussed in this book. Being present is simple enough, but it is not easy to accomplish. The work you put into it is absolutely necessary, however, as it is a goal that *must* be achieved.

This idea of living in the moment goes against what we may have learned in the past where we are asked to focus everything we have into things like our careers. However, living in the moment, or being mindful (as it has become known in the mainstream), could be the only ticket we need to a fuller, happier, more positive life.

There is a term called multitasking. It is supposedly the ability to do more than one thing at a time, or the ability to handle multiple assignments—not related to each other—effectively. Now, I hate to be the bearer of bad news, but there's no such thing as multitasking efficiently!

These days, when we are listing special skills on our work resumes, we have to state that we can multi-task as that puts us in a better position to obtain work due to the western tradition that we have all adopted. The 9-to-5 grind seems to require everyone to be made from the same cookie cutter, and every hiring manager is looking for these similar words written on that meaningless piece of paper...

The thing with this method of life is that in truth, multi-tasking robs us of our ability to be present because when we multi-task, we are never paying full attention to any of the tasks at hand. While we are preparing a letter, we are thinking of the meeting we are to attend to later. While in the meeting, we are focusing on the report that is to be submitted later, and there are also thoughts of argument we had with someone yesterday, what to make for dinner, and if we will make it to the train in time for work tomorrow.

Unfortunately, most of us are never truly mentally present.

"When walking, walk;
when eating, eat."
-Zen Proverb

We should act deliberately. We should try to do things because we want to, not because we have to. Acting out of necessity creates a *hurried* feeling where we are thinking of consequences rather than the actual thing we are doing.

Acting out of our own deliberation helps us to focus on the task at hand.

Don't forget to take breaks. Your mind needs time to reset on a regular basis, especially during work days or during big projects.

When you have been at your desk for a couple of hours, rest it out for five to ten minutes. In this time, think of nothing, keep a clear mind and just be. This calms you up and frees you for the next phase of work.

Great thinkers in the past practiced something called polyphonic sleep, where they got 20 minutes of sleep for every three hours of being awake.

This is not a realistic pattern in the kind of lifestyle we have adopted today, but as an alternative, take regular breaks and free your mind from thinking.

This creates clarity, improves memory, and aids focus.

Convert your less busy time to your quiet time. When you are cooking, perhaps you can use that time to reflect. When you get home from a busy day, perhaps take a moment to practice gratitude. Imagine what you want to achieve, generate feelings of positivity, meditate.

It can begin with a few simple minutes a day, and those few minutes can change everything.

> *"Once upon a time is really here and now."*
> *-Anonymous*

It is never too late to unlearn the unconstructive habits we have picked up along the way, all that is necessary is to possess the will to make a change, and then we can.

Each day that we practice being present and living in the now, we are tapping into our inner magic and filling that now with pure, light and happy positivity.

Practice Your Power Exercise:

Let us teach ourselves how to be present. Start by turning off your cell phone the next time you are with family. Turn off the TV when you are about to read. Set a screen time lock on your phone for certain apps that are distracting. Block out time for work and time for play.

Focus on a specific task at a specific time. This builds your focus and ability to do things in a shorter time. This makes you plan better and execute more efficiently.

Start small, and build up to longer times when you are aware that you are fully present to the task or activity at hand.

Ask yourself many times throughout the day,

"What am I doing right now?"

An example is that you may be eating. When you become present while eating, this helps you enjoy the taste and nourishment that meal is giving you at that time.

If you are present while driving for example, you become a better driver, more aware of the road you are on.

The more present you are, the more you are mastering your mindset. But don't be worried if you slip back into your old habits! That's normal. Just recognize it, and then change your mindset again. Remember, you are the one in control of your mind. What you think, you become.

The quote below is something I heard many years ago and although I understood it when I heard it, it actually took me a long time before I fully knew what it meant.

We have this incredible ability to create our own magic, our own moments. And it starts with here and now. It starts with you.

> *"The present moment is the only moment available to us, and it is the door to all moments."*
> *-Nhat Hanh*

STEP ELEVEN

SURROUNDINGS

"You cannot hang out with negative people and expect to live a positive life."
-Joel Osteen

There are no coincidences in life. The places we are born into always turn out to be the place that will make for our best primary growth. There is no disputing this. Along the way, however, we start learning to make decisions, and our decisions start to shape our future, and so on.

I hope you are beginning to learn, as I have on my path to self-creation, that we are not a product of our environment but rather our environment is a reflection of us. What surrounds us at any point in time is the result of our past thoughts and decisions, just as the thoughts and decisions taken today will mold what surrounds us tomorrow.

Our surroundings are always giving us feedback as to where we are in our emotional and thought world, so, you can see why it is important to pay attention to our environment. Our surroundings may very well be our best teachers in regards to what we need to start or stop doing. Bad choices in friends for example, can lead to negativity coming into our lives on a daily basis.

Perhaps we end up hanging out with these negative influences because they are our 'friends', and we end up in bad neighborhoods, doing things that don't really make us feel very good about ourselves... Or we slowly begin to lower our own standards of morals.

When I am talking about surroundings, it goes beyond the houses, trees, and climate in your environment. It includes, in great extent, to the people in your environment.

We are the equivalent of the five people we spend most of our time with. Are these people you want to be like? Do they inspire you? Respect you? Motivate you? Encourage you? Celebrate your successes? Cheer you on? Do you admire their success? Can you learn from them? Are they working on building their own best quality of life?

If not, then it's time to re-think how much time you want to spend with them.

There is a saying I have shared with you below that, in one sentence, explains the pure impact of the people we choose to surround ourselves with.

"Show me who your friends are, and I will show you who you are."
-Anonymous

This is very true, because the minds and people you connect with ultimately become you. You cannot surround yourself with armed robbers and not get caught in the cross fire. It works the same in the opposite regard, you cannot surround yourself with successful people and remain unsuccessful.

Please do yourself a favor and take this as encouragement. Take it as a knowledge that you can choose what your environment is, even when sometimes you feel stuck. Eventually you will have the willpower to change.

A country, city, or community is a collective reflection of the dominant mind set of the people residing there. So even though your mind is active and the place is a reflection of who you are, when you start to grow, some environments will no longer 'fit' you and you can tell that you are outgrowing that place.

Think of it as a child who is a growing physically. She gets a pair of pants and they fit so well, but after six months the pants start to shrink. At first, she doesn't realize that she is growing. She starts to wonder why a perfectly good set of trousers would lose their fitting all of a sudden.

After some more months it is obviously awkward anytime she puts on that particular piece of clothing, and until it is replaced, she will not be comfortable wearing them. They are too tight, too short and no longer fit her.

A good exercise to practice is to constantly weigh your feelings against your surroundings.

Ask yourself,

"How do I feel about the place I am right now?"

We find that it is common for people to criticize the government for all personal or communal issues the people of that country may have.

This happens in so many countries, yet a person who is able to see past blame and search for truth will quickly realize that the government of any given place is simply a reflection of the mass mind living there.

Surely the government is not reflecting 100% of the people in that place, but we here use the term 'dominant'.

Life Story:

Miguel grew up in the poverty ridden city of Chiapas, Mexico. As he got older, he noticed a lot of issues in the society as he improved his own mind set and grew as an individual.

He noticed that the majority of the people there had poor environmental habits. Those sweeping the roads would push the garbage into the gutters. Those enjoying a snack in their cars would wind down their windows and discard their empty bottles and snack packets on the road, making it filthy. Some people in that city were even in the habit of urinating by the road side.

Yet, after all these unhygienic actions of the people, they would always blame the government for not maintaining hygiene in the city.

Even after the government had designated refuse dumping spots around the city, the people there would not tie up their garbage as instructed, and the place would look like a mess before the clean-up team would get there.

Miguel went to visit British Colombia, Canada at some point in his life while on business, and he realized it was a different ball game over there.

The people were so orderly and coordinated, but what caught his initial attention was how clean the place was. He went to other provinces as well, like Alberta and Ontario, and he noticed that these places were very clean too—that the people there were law abiding and sanitation-conscious.

They put their garbage into trash cans that were placed on many street corners. They had a stronger presence of law enforcement so there were no people taking to the streets to urinate. It became obvious that the issue he noticed with the city he grew up in was solely that city's problem. Not the problem of their entire country, nor the issues of the government.

If you find that the mass-mind of your environment is in opposition with your own thought process, then the way out is to quietly exempt yourself from that environment, not complain or stage protests against it.

If you are in a decision-making position, then you are free to put things in place to improve the mentality of the people living there. But other than that, a quiet exit would serve you and every other person.

> *"When we are no longer able to change the situation, we are challenged to change ourselves."*
> *-Viktor E. Frankl*

Trying to help people who don't want to be helped can drain you of your own positivity. You cannot force others to change. That is one thing I have learned for an absolute truth in my life, through many, many trials and errors! We all know at least one person that we believe has so much potential, but no matter what we say to them, or try to teach them, they do not change.

Through the highs and the lows of the many relationships in my life with friends, family and partners, the enduring truth is that if someone is not willing to change, they will not. And there is nothing you can do about it. You must learn to let it go, and move forward and be at peace with the fact that YOU are growing, and that is what truly matters.

Once you decide to better your surroundings and yourself, you must then also decide to let go of the people who maintain your old lifestyle and refuse to grow. Sometimes this can be painful, as it can be family members who you may realize are bringing out negative events in your own life, or lifelong friends.

Making a choice to create a better life for yourself is not selfish, it is a true personal blessing, and can be quite a challenge. But trust me, once you start to better your surroundings, you will decide for yourself not to allow fear to force you to look back.

You will find that as you grow and notice your surroundings, with little or no effort, you will be drawn to the places that you align with, and which would help you be the best you that you can be.

You will find that new people, places and situations present themselves to you in order for you to reach your goals. The more you focus on your new way of thinking, your new life and your goals... the more you will achieve and the more powerful you will feel.

You will begin to draw in your positive new life, bringing with it all the energy you need to create your dream world. Now that is true MAGIC from within yourself.

Practice Your Power Exercise:

Write down a list of the people in your life right now. Friends, family, acquaintances, romantic partners, colleagues, anyone that you spend time with on a regular basis. Now beside their name, write how this person makes you feel when you're around them. Write down the type of person they are, the attitude they have, their outlook on life. Are they positive or negative? Are they always complaining or are they always sharing happy stories? Are they successful or are they always jus scraping by and never wanting to change?

If the people you surround yourself with are negative or are bringing toxicity into your life, you need to make a choice to either remove them from your life, or to set up strong healthy boundaries with them so that their negative traits don't corrupt the positive lifestyle you are working so hard to develop for yourself right now.

It doesn't matter if that person is your mother or your best friend you've had for 20 years - if you come to realize that they are having a negative impact on your life, you need to protect yourself and set up clear boundaries.

Next write down the environment you find yourself in. This can be your home, your place of work, the city you live in, and so on. Now beside each one, write down how it makes you feel. Are you happy where you live? Are you comfortable at your job? Does the city you live in give you the ability to achieve the success you want?

This second batch will be a bit harder to change, because they are big things like your home and work place. But the simple act of acknowledging how you really feel about them and the impact they have on your life will enable you to consciously begin to make changes towards a more positive environment.

As you change your surroundings, you will change your life on such a big scale that I am truly excited to hear how you feel once you remove what doesn't serve you and start drawing in what does!

"You cannot change or control the people around you, but you can decide who you have around
you and who you no longer want in your life."
-Sarah Hall

STEP TWELVE

GIVING

"No act of kindness, no matter how small, is ever wasted."
-Aesop

When I have more for myself, then I will be able to give back. Until then, I need this for myself to survive. That is a thought pattern that, unfortunately, has eaten deep into the minds of the people in this world. If you catch yourself thinking this, then heed my words—you will never have enough to give, and you will never have everything you desire in your life. Never.

We all know the definition of giving, however, due to orientation or our upbringing, we may not know the essence or the advantage of giving.

We are all connected in this world and what that means is that whatever we give to each other, we give to ourselves.

When I mention giving, it is usual to think that all we can give are tangible gifts—things we can hold and touch. But that is seldom the case. We will revisit that in a little bit. There are also many times we feel that we have nothing to give. At such times as this, you would be surprised at what you can let go of in order to improve another person's life.

"When you feel helpless; help someone."
-Anonymous

My sister Tamara was a giver. She was blessed to learn early on in life that giving should be a lifestyle.

She was taught to give love and kindness to others, unconditionally, no matter their status, their background or their lifestyle choice.

Let me clarify, she wasn't taught to overextend herself, but to be kind and loving whenever possible, not to people who were out to hurt her, but to people in general.

Tamara had adapted to this mode of thought and she shone like a brilliant star because it was her nature to give, even if all she had to give was her beautiful smile. She had been told by some peers that her attitude would lead to people taking advantage of her.

Yet, Tamara never cared about this. She never worried that people wouldn't be kind to her in return. She gave for the love of giving, not because she wanted something in return. She gave the world her heart, and she was kind to anyone, and everyone, no matter where they came from. And people loved my sister so much for her huge heart. She was a beacon of joy in so many people's lives, and she is missed so much since her passing.

That, my friends, is the true essence of giving. It comes from your heart and it sends out a bright light and a free form of energy—a magic that lifts others up and makes them feel loved in return.

We should know that giving is a choice and to give if it feels right. There is a joy that comes from being able to offer help to someone in need.

There is also a great reward that stems from giving. However, you rob yourself of that reward when you give to others only because you are expecting something in return from them.

Parable:

In the land of the animals, a long time ago, all animals got along and were great pals. They lived together and all was well. One day the antelope was wandering and he got lost. She walked and walked till she got to a dead end. Since she did not know where to go, she started crying.

When she cried, a portal opened up and she saw a mysterious being. It asked her why she was crying and she explained that she was lost, that she needed to get back to her home.

The mysterious being would not return her to her home unless the antelope gave something in return. The antelope said she had nothing to give, and the mysterious being responded that she must give something, no matter how small.

The antelope thought for a moment and said all she had to give was her voice. She was a good singer. The mysterious being agreed to the gift, and after singing, a portal was opened for the antelope with a big basket of gifts which she was told not to open until she got home. The antelope thanked the mysterious being and headed home.

On arrival, she opened the basket and all manner of expensive jewelry sprung forth. The antelope was instantly rich and she threw the biggest party the town had ever seen. She used her gifts to enrich the lives of others and gave to the needy.

Upon seeing the good fortune of the antelope, the tortoise thought he could also benefit from this, so he went to the antelope and asked how it all happened.

Being a friend to the tortoise, the antelope relayed the whole story in detail. After listening, the tortoise decided he was going to claim his own wealth.

After careful deliberation, one morning the tortoise set out. He mapped out his steps till he got to the dead end. Then he started crying, hoping the mysterious being will magically show itself. As expected, the magical creature appeared and asked him why he was crying. He claimed he was lost and that he needed to find his way home.

The mysterious being asked if he had something to trade for his return and the tortoise said yes. He had withdrawn all his money from his debtors so he could have enough to give—of course, he reasoned that the more you give, the more you get.

He already visualized how big his basket would be as he emptied his bag and poured all his belongings on the ground in front of the magical creature.

The mysterious being gave him a much bigger bag than what he gave to the antelope and told him to keep it closed until he got back to his village. The tortoise was so happy and though he could barely lift the bag, he pulled with all his might and took it out of there.

As soon as the creature was out of site, the tortoise hurried to open the bag. In it he found the biggest, fiercest, ugliest creature he had ever seen... and that was how the tortoise's life ended.

This story is usually the case with the bulk of people who have had the wrong orientation in respect to giving.

They cannot give without expecting something in return. And giving only because you expect something in return is really not giving at all. That kind of giving always comes back to haunt us.

So, what exactly can you give?

Time

Spend some time with people under seven and over seventy. See the smile on their faces as you help them get through a particular task. Make sure to let them complete the task, so they know they are capable, and watch their faces light up as you assist them.

Give your time to charities, to churches, to hospitals. Hand out hot food to the less fortunate. Dress up like a superhero and go to your local children's hospital and make a child laugh, make their day brighter.

Find a cause that makes you feel good for helping, and volunteer in any way that you can. Get your friends involved, or go alone! Get out of your comfort zone and start giving back. You will feel amazing, trust me.

Spend some time with your family and friends that you don't see often. Volunteer at a senior's home, or a homeless shelter, or an animal shelter. Give your time to society and embrace how it feels to be a part of a bigger cause.

Talent/Skill

What is it you can do for someone? Do you have a beautiful voice? Or a passion for singing? Maybe you can sing someone out of a bad mood!

Are you funny? A comedian? Really good at telling stories? Then you can make people laugh when they are sad! You can spread joy to others.

Are you great with a paint brush? An artist? Then you can help someone paint their new apartment, or give someone a beautiful homemade gift of a portrait.

Are you a musician? Play an instrument? Then you can teach someone else how to play a tune!

Maybe you are an incredible public speaker and can motivate others, so go and set up a free course to teach others your life lessons!

Are you a writer? Write someone a love letter, a thank-you note, a grateful little message that shows them you care.

Use your skills to develop the skills of another person, this is a great way to give back.

Love

Practice giving your love deeply, freely and meaningfully. Let love be your center. Learn to embrace love, to give love and to express gratitude freely. This is the magic you have, use it.

Make someone feel appreciated, give an honest compliment. Uplift someone with kind words of encouragement and hope.

Do as my sister Tamara always did, and give someone your truest smile, filled with love, to brighten their day.

The littlest act of love can pull someone out of the darkest space in their life. We do not know how much impact we can have on a person's life until we give it a try. So, try it today, spread love like a virus! It's contagious and it's good for you.

Practice giving love daily, giving it freely, and I promise you that you will begin to fill more love flowing into your life from every avenue. The more love you give, the more you have to give, and the more you will get in return!

Just like magic.

Money

Most times just a few dollars are all a person needs to have hope again. Sure, money is physical, but it is a means. The things you can do with money are endless.

Pay someone's hospital bills. Pay a person's transport fare. Buy someone in need their lunch or dinner.

In the summer time, I always buy cases of water bottles and keep them in my car to hand out to less fortunate people who I see begging on the street corners by traffic lights—it's hot and they are out there all day.

You may find however that money is harder to give because everybody needs it in one way or another.

You might find yourself hoarding money because you never seem to have enough. But once you begin giving back, no matter how little it is at first, you will find that more money will flow freely into your life. Don't hoard money, it's not truly yours to begin with!

Pay for the person's coffee in the drive through behind you. If you're asked to donate to charity, do it. Even when you only have $5 in your bank account, give $2 to the homeless shelter. That $2 might not end up meaning anything to you, yet it could be everything for someone less fortunate.

Joy

This doesn't seem like a big deal, right? Well it is!

A cheerful disposition is one of the best things a person can give. It is literally impossible to see a nice smile and not return it. Try it and you would see that it is true.

We have talked about smiling all through this book, and although there is a saying that goes, "Smiling doesn't pay the bills," I strongly beg to differ. A smile is the beginning of a whole lot of things.

And I must say, if smiling does not pay bills, remember that frowning doesn't pay those bills either! No one ever got farther ahead by being a miserable so-and-so.

Give someone a genuine compliment. Remember how you felt when that nice, random lady at the supermarket commented on how pretty your new sundress was? Remember how amazing it made you feel? Be that person! Compliment others!

So be cheerful. Be positive. Spread that positivity around like it's contagious, like it's a magical spell that you can share with everyone around you, and great things will happen for you. I guarantee it.

Good Thoughts

Of course, we can't instantly see our thoughts manifesting, but we can feel them. And trust me, those thoughts go a long way. Practice sending good thoughts out to even those who don't like you. You will be a better person for it, and you will begin to shift your mindset and karma to the positive side of the number line. It's not easy at first, but it becomes easier soon.

In some societies in the world, people are happy when they hear that others have suffered misfortunes or losses. That should never be the case. It's time for a permanent perception shift. Those who have wronged us in the past can be forgiven, and we now wish them well. Love and release, then move forward.

Each morning, when you are writing out your grateful list, include a friend, a family member, a co-worker, or maybe even someone you don't particularly like very much.

Write one good quality he/she has which you are grateful for. Wish someone a quick recovery in the case of an illness.

Literally wish other people well. Be happy for, and celebrate when you hear about something good happening to someone else.

Cast away envy. Envy and jealousy are the seeds of all failure! They are like a disease that can deteriorate any progress you're having for yourself.

The more you think about what others have, and are jealous or frustrated that you do not have those things yet, the farther away you are pushing yourself from getting those things!

Send out good thoughts, congratulate others on their successes, and send positive thoughts and kindness out each and every day.

Practice Your Power Exercise:

Write a list of the things you have that you can give. Is it a skill you have? Are you able to donate to a charitable cause? Can you give your time as a volunteer?

Now do a bit of research and find ways to put this into action. If you can't start big, start small. I promise you that no matter who you are, or where you are in your life right now – you have something to give. And there are people out there who need you. You have the power to change someone's life, that's how powerful you are. Don't squander it.

"You cannot give what you don't have, but to have, you must first give."
-Chinese Proverb

RESPECT YOURSELF

Respect yourself enough to walk away from anything that no longer serves to make you happy.

Self-respect is not conceit or narcissism. It is a healthy regard for who you are.

In life we always find ourselves in one relationship or another. It could be a relationship with our parents, or siblings, friends from school, romantic relationships, or with co-workers.

The point is, relationships are something we all find ourselves in, regardless of who we are. And in a relationship, it is so easy to lose sight of important things and start disrespecting ourselves.

It could be that we find ourselves in a job that goes against our purpose, but because our friend got us that job, we stay in it because we don't want to hurt our friend.

Yet what we don't always appreciate is that every second we spend doing something we don't like, we are disrespecting ourselves, and once you are disrespecting yourself, you cannot be positive. Things like depression, anger, defensiveness and other heavy feelings are a sign of self-disrespect.

Earlier we spoke about being comfortable with who you are. If we are not comfortable with ourselves, others will get a feel of that and it can put strains on relationships or cause us to project negativity, even when we do not mean to.

I have noticed this in myself in the past.

An example of this would be when I am not feeling my best and someone says something that I immediately take the wrong way, and I become defensive.

Now, I notice when that is happening and I can catch myself, and take a second to relax.

Then I ask myself:

"What is making me unhappy right now?"

And then I can fix it, instead of taking it out on others.

For the purpose of enlightenment and evaluation, I am going to explain a few signs to recognize in yourself, in order to see if you are disrespecting yourself.

By examining yourself based on these signs, you can have a perspective on the direction you are headed towards.

Anger

There is something interesting about anger. Rather than be a destructive factor, we could use it as a guide.

When something annoys you, it means something needs to change. But all change starts with us. All change must come from within. That is a part of our inner magic, we are the only ones capable of creating that change within ourselves.

You are more powerful than you think you are.

Remember that.

There could also be an annoying situation but you realize that you are not fazed by it, it doesn't bother you in the slightest. What this means is that it is someone else's lesson to learn.

Yet when you are annoyed by the situation (irrespective of what caused that annoyance), you have something to change, and it may be hard to swallow, but it is the truth. This method can be a life-saving thought.

So, the next time you feel anger creeping up, ask yourself, "Why am I angry?" and "What can I do to prevent this situation from repeating itself?"

Better yet, ask yourself, "What can I do so that if this situation repeats itself, I do not get angry?"

The answers will definitely come.

My sister Tamara always used to say, "Trust farm heavy." It was her way of saying "Trust me, I know the way."

This is an appropriate time for me to say that, so listen young grasshopper, trust farm heavy, and I assure you that the answers will always reveal themselves.

Seeking Approval from Others

To seek approval from someone, or something else, simply means that we do not have enough self-respect to believe in what we have done, or in what we are doing. I want you to recognize that seeking approval and asking an honest opinion are two very different things.

When we seek approval, it is a desperate action. Our mood seems to be affected, or worse yet, our mood is even dictated by the feedback we get from others. This is not healthy behavior and it is definitely a sign that we are disrespecting ourselves. When we feel others need to approve us, we rob ourselves of the freedom that comes with being our own person.

We end up stifling our creativity and we doom ourselves. So, I am asking you right this moment, here and now, to let go of that need to be approved by others. We can do that by remembering our awesomeness.

Because remember:

Irrespective of the past, I AM AWESOME.

We will become less anxious and more creative as we do this for ourselves daily. Love yourself for who you are and don't let anyone dictate your magic.

Letting Others Dictate Your Life

This is closely related to the previous point though with a little twist. We just learned that we let other people's opinions count more than they should, and here we talk about letting other people become our 'controllers'.

Bringing it closer to home, we have parents deciding who and when their children should marry or what career paths they should take. Sometimes we even have friends who jump on the opportunity to decide what jobs you would be good at, should apply to, and so on.

We can't live positively, and we cannot master our mindset if we have other people making our decisions for us. The reason is because when someone makes a decision, it is based on the experiences of the person making the decision, not the person they are making it for.

Yet someone else can never truly understand what our own personal experiences are in life, so they do not know what is truly best for us. Seeing it this way, you will understand that we become our own best coaches in life.

We know what we want out of our lives, we are learning how to create that for ourselves by utilizing our inner magic, and we know now that we know what is best for our true selves.

> *"Don't let the behavior of others destroy your inner peace."*
> *-Dalai Lama*

My preferred way to say this is: Don't let idiots ruin your day! There are always going to be people who want to project their fears, stresses and their own negative self-talk on you.

Don't absorb it. Don't take it onboard. Don't let them ruin your day. Let it bounce off and you just move on to be your amazing self.

Being Hard on Yourself

Whether or not we like it, or accept it, we will, at some point, make mistakes. Happy people accept that. Every mistake is an opportunity to learn something new, or as Henry Ford put it:

"A chance to try again, smarter."

We have all been hard on ourselves. I know I am guilty of this, even when I am focused on doing my best. Something might happen and before I know it, I find I am criticizing myself. I have to mentally check myself at these moments. I have to stop and accept what happened, recognize it's in the past, know that I cannot change the past and move forward.

Beating ourselves up over something—even if it's some huge disastrous mistake or accident—won't change anything. But you know what it will do? It will make it worse. You will *feel* worse. You will feel a mixture of negative emotions towards yourself, such as sadness, anger, or self-hate, and thinking those things is like spreading a sort of toxic negativity inside your own self.

When you find yourself in a hole, stop digging. When you find yourself on the floor, get back up.

That is how it works. Stop keeping score.

Move on and try again. Forgiving yourself for each mistake you make is the first step to allowing others to be forgiving of your mistakes.

Free yourself of the cumbersome responsibility of beating yourself up for something you have done, or have refused, or forgotten to do.

Rejecting Your Intuition

Instincts are real. Your own instincts can teach you so much about yourself and the decisions you're making.

You may have come to notice that every once in a while, you hear that voice, or that inner nudging, which urges you to do, or to stop doing something.

When we follow it, we realize that things go smoothly. When we don't follow it, we see that there is something we would have gained if we did. Other times we may find that there is something we have been saved from—some disaster averted—because we listened to that nudging.

When we listen, the voice gets louder to the point where we can't help but listen. And when we ignore our instincts, the voice gets quieter till we can no longer hear it. No matter how silly it sounds, follow that nudging and keep true to your instincts, because that little voice inside you is a deep seeded part of the magic within you.

Take it seriously, but not too seriously.

Your instincts would never ask you to jump off a bridge, for example. Let your instincts ask for small things, help you make little decisions along the way as you conquer this path called life.

It doesn't hurt to listen. In fact, it could actually save and improve our quality of life. Your basic intuition is an excellent guiding voice to whether something or someone makes you feel good, or bad. Whether a situation is positive, or negative.

Talking Down on Yourself

This usually starts out small. Maybe you're beating yourself up just a little bit about something silly you've just said or done, but it can spiral out of control before you realize what's going on.

You might have said something like this:

- I am not good enough.
- I am not sure that I can.
- I cannot afford it.
- I am going to mess it up.
- I am going to be late.
- I am going to fail.
- I am not good at anything.
- I am not smart enough.

These thoughts do not help you, and they certainly shouldn't be part of your daily thinking pattern.

These thoughts are those of self-pity.

So, in reality, each time one of these thoughts come into our mind, our positivity diminishes when we indulge in them.

The next time you hear such thoughts coming through, give yourself a positive affirmation that is the complete opposite:

- I am good enough.
- I can do this.
- I have more than enough money.
- I am amazing.
- I have more than enough time.
- I am a winner.
- I am good at everything I put my mind to.
- I am smart and talented.

Doesn't it feel better to give yourself a short, yet sweet, positive affirmation?

You will find that saying affirmations becomes easier, and the more you say them to yourself—either out loud, or in your head—the more magic you will create inside yourself.

The more confidence you will instill inside yourself. The more you will begin to believe in what you're affirming!

"You will never know how far you'll fly if you don't spread your wings and jump. Tell yourself there's no more holding back...
and take the leap!"
−Sarah Hall

Let me tell you about how using positive affirmations has helped me build my own successes in life, little by little. I make it a mental note each day while I am driving to work to say right out loud in my car this affirmation:

"I have more than enough money, I have money coming in. I love money and money loves me!"

I say that affirmation every day, even on those tough days when I was behind on bills. When I was using my last $10 to put gas in my tank so I can get to work. When I couldn't afford to pay my rent of time and risked losing my house. Especially at those times.

Do you know why? Because when you feel like you're running on empty, those are the times when you need positive affirmations the most. They will work if you truly believe in them.

I find that when I tell myself that "I have more than enough money, I have money coming in. I love money and money loves me!" I am more productive that day, I reach more people, I make a bigger impact.

I actually make MORE money because I have affirmed in my own mind that I already DO make more money, and that I have more than enough money. And when I do find myself with extra income, or a bonus check, or more money in my bank account than I thought I had, I am grateful.

I express my gratitude and welcome more into my life with open arms. Because money isn't a bad thing. We all use it to live! And if you want a good life, then you need to work more on appreciating money, and less on thinking thoughts like "money is the root of all evil," etc.

I tell myself that I am successful and that good things are happening, even when they aren't. Because affirming in my mind that good things are happening CREATES good things to happen.

Are you catching on yet?

When I affirm with positive statements, I have great days. People are drawn to me like bees to flowers. I can actually feel myself vibrating on a higher level and it excites me. It's that special magic within us all that has taught me that I can control my own destiny and I create my own life.

You know the saying; bad things happen in threes? By believing something like that you will actually make more bad things happen in your life.

Like a vicious cycle.

When you dwell on negative thoughts, you create more negative thoughts. You become a breeding ground for bad things to happen to you.

Switching out negative, destructive statements for positive affirmations builds our energy as we speak these positive things to ourselves.

Remember that out of the fullness of the heart, the mouth speaks. This means that every negative word spoken must have first been conceived as a thought. So, before the thought manifests in words, replace it with a positive one!

Keeping Quiet When Hurt

This is not the same as complaining. If someone is hurting us, they should know what they are doing. Most times we endure maltreatment for no just cause. We should be able to speak for ourselves and let them know that they are being hurtful.

Perhaps they don't know and by speaking up and talking about it, we can help them change their behavior. If we let others know and they are obstinate, and do not change the hurtfulness of their actions or words, it is left to us to remove ourselves from the position that encourages the maltreatment.

If someone continues to treat you poorly even after you have given them a chance to change, then it's time to say goodbye. You deserve better than that. You truly do! Just walk away.

It doesn't matter who they are to you: family, friends, or co-workers. Just distance yourself from that kind of toxic behavior and you will be stronger for it.

We teach our children to stand up to bullies, but we find that a lot of adults allow themselves to be bullied in the name of money, positions, and relationships. Take a stand, put an end to it.

This goes deeper too if someone has done something to you that's abusive, whether that abuse is sexual, emotional or physical. You give someone power over you when you keep quiet. You are sacrificing a part of yourself to protect someone who does not deserve protection. If someone has hurt you, speak out about it.

Tell your partner, your trusted friends, your parents, your doctor, whoever you need to in order to get the help that you require and in order to prevent that person from hurting you again, or from going on to hurt others. If you keep quiet then you could be allowing a predator to continue hurting more people, please speak out and allow your voice to be heard. Take your power back and you can begin to heal.

Judgmental Attitude

We define 'judgmental' as having an overly critical point of view. When we realize that we are quick to point out the fault in others, we find that we are edging towards that judgmental place.

We should always try to hear everyone's story with a clear mind, without the cloud of judgement, before we decipher for ourselves what is and what isn't.

There is a saying and it goes, "Be wary of those who gossip to you, for they will gossip of you."

This is an incredibly true statement.

People who spread rumors and gossip will inevitably share your secrets, or speak negatively about you behind your back.

It's just the type of person they are. So, do yourself a favor and don't indulge them when they come to you with the latest gossip about someone. It doesn't do anything positive in your life to hear about the misfortunes of others, and it certainly doesn't do you any good to talk about others negatively!

On that note, I feel it's important to mention that when you have a friend or family member (or even an acquaintance) tell you something in confidence, keep that confidence. Respect them, respect their privacy, and keep it to yourself. They trusted you, so let that trust be well founded and you will be a better person for it.

Unless of course it involves something that should be reported to the police or involves their well-being or health. In that case you should immediately seek help for them.

Spending Time with Negative People

Our self-worth is important and should never be overlooked, underrated or toyed around with. The first voice we listen to is our own, but the next voice that we listen to is the voice of those we spend the bulk of our time with, be it our family, our spouse, or our friends.

You may have a friend who you've known for years, and maybe they are a great friend in many aspects, yet every time you speak to them, you feel their negative energy rubbing off on you. Maybe you get a call from them and all they do is complain, always a new dramatic story to tell.

Maybe they speak poorly of others, or they are constantly in a downward spiral and don't take any advice—they never try to better their own situation or help themselves.

Unfortunately, this is toxic for you. This person doesn't realize what they are doing to their own lives, and you are in the process of trying to create a better and more positive life for yourself, so you should distance yourself from them.

Now, I know many of us don't want to create space between ourselves and our friends, or even family, that have been a part of our lives for so long. So, another tactic for dealing with a negative person can be to only share good news with them, and not respond to, or feed into any negative news, opinions, or attitudes they share with you.

Perhaps they will come around, perhaps they will see your life changing for the better and they will begin to wonder if they are capable of doing that for themselves. I've seen it before, people can change. IF they want to change.

When we spend time with people who don't appreciate us, we are not in any way helping ourselves. When we spend time with those who disrespect us, even when they don't mean to, we eat away at our core and become less of who we are.

If we want to create a great life for ourselves, we cannot continue to surround ourselves with negative people. You are who you hang out with.

Remember:

WE ARE AWESOME
WE ARE POWERFUL
WE HAVE MAGIC WITHIN US

…and quite frankly, anyone who does not support that line of thought is not worthy of spending time with us.

PERIOD.

THE MAGIC PATH

"If you want to change your life you need to plant the seeds
of success within yourself and nourish them daily."
-Sarah Hall

Let us now look at some things that show us that we are going
in the right direction on the magic path to our new positive
lifestyle. You may feel at first that once you begin thinking
positively and exercising your inner magic, that everything else
will just fall into place automatically.

I know for myself that when I first starting putting these steps
into motion in my own life years ago, I was certain that all my
biggest dreams would just manifest themselves almost instantly.
That's not how positive magic works. But it does set forth the
wheels into motion. For example, I wanted a BMW for many
years, since I first got my driver's license. Yet a BMW was
expensive and I didn't have the means to get one.

I kept that dream alive over the years by admiring BMW's when I saw them around, asking dealerships I attended if they had any new ones in stock, talking about BMW's with my friends, and even having a photo of a BMW on my vision board in my office.

It didn't happen overnight, because that's a pretty big thing to desire, but I was never desperate for it. In fact, before I got my BMW, I bought another car entirely! It was a car that I loved very much (a Mitsubishi Spyder Eclipse convertible) and I drove it everywhere.

I've taken that car on many incredible road trips, made tons of great memories with it. In fact, I used that car for 6 years, and I took good care of it. I put new tires on, kept the gas tank filled, and took it for yearly check-ups and oil changes.

It wasn't the BMW I was dreaming of, but it was what the Universe presented to me at that point in my life, and I was eternally grateful for it!

Remember earlier when I explained about how desire works hand in hand with gratitude?

In order to allow more into your life, you must first be thankful for what you have. If you treat each thing you currently have with respect and appreciation, then you will set the wheels in motion to attract more into your life.

This is the abundance factor.

It works like MAGIC.

In fact, I bought my very own BMW the same year I wrote this book—2016 and it was an incredible feeling. After years of visualizing, working hard and appreciating what I already had, my desire and my gratitude worked together to manifest the car I have always wanted. This is the law of attraction at its finest. It starts with YOU. And without you, it's nothing.

A car is only a silly, material thing that I use as an example here, but there are so many ways to use this incredible magic to draw into your life what you want and desire.

When you use your inner magic to manifest your desires, and turn your dreams into reality, the Universe will change people, places and things to assist you with that manifestation. It works, like magic.

You need to nurture your ability to manifest. That will take growth through learning, and much practice. Growth is a constant process, and when we grow, sometimes it hurts at first. Think of it like exercise, it hurts until you get used to it.

It can be painful or difficult when you start an activity that you are not used to, such as working out, or mindfulness, or playing the piano.

Do you remember teething? It's the point in every human's life when they start to grow new teeth, and just in case we have forgotten, it hurts a lot and is uncomfortable.

There are several emotions that may come up now that you have decided to live in this new powerfully positive way. You may notice as you're reading that you have already experienced some of these feelings in the past, but perhaps you have forgotten what it felt like at that time, just as you may have forgotten what it felt like to be teething as a baby.

I want to explain each of those feelings to you, so that you can better understand that they are normal. That you are strong enough to overcome them all and live with your inner magic shining bright.

Feeling Fear of Your New Path

Don't let the fear of potential failure rule your life and thoughts. Whenever we are staring something new, that fear tries to creep in. We say, "I have learned these steps, and now I want to practice positivity, but what if I fail?"

This is common and we have all been there. Even our first day in any school is a bit tense.

Now I encourage you to meet these new uncomfortable feelings with enthusiasm. It is only with enthusiasm and hopefulness that we can push that fear aside. So, what if we fail? It's not the end of the world! To err is human.

We will learn from how we handled the situation, and we will try again. But why should we fail? We have read such an awesome book as this, and we are feeling fired up and ready. We have nothing to lose. Right? Right!

Keep your attitude positive, and when you feel fear coming up, simply acknowledge and welcome that fear, but tell it right to its face that it's not in the driver's seat, and it can't watch the road maps or give directions any longer.

You can let fear know that it's always going to be there, because it will. It's part of our human nature to feel fear. But fear isn't allowed to rule any longer. You're in charge from here on out.

Feeling There Isn't Enough Time

You might think that you will not succeed because of the feeling that there is not enough time.

When we want to start a new project, we give ourselves timelines (you noticed I didn't use the word 'deadlines', as a deadline creates a negative energy towards the project. Avoid using the word 'dead' in relation to projects you're working on!).

The strange thing, however, is once that timeline is set, time seems to move very quickly.

We start to feel there is not enough time to do the things we have said we want to accomplish, and the temptation to procrastinate becomes very strong. I know for myself, if I don't set a timeline or plan out a project properly, then I find myself constantly pushing it back to 'another day'.

The thing about positive power is that when you tell yourself you will do something 'another day', that day will never come. When you set goals, focus on them every day! Even the littlest thought about your goal counts as a projection of energy towards its accomplishment.

So, if you feel there isn't enough time, remind yourself that it is just a test to see if we will persevere in the direction we have chosen.

We are to remember that time is an illusion, and that what is actually important is the vision we have in our minds. That vision is for a better life, and the power to create it for ourselves. Keep focused on that.

Feeling Intolerant of Negative People

Yes, this is a big one.

You might find yourself lecturing a friend because they still talk in negative ways, with negative mannerisms. You might suddenly find that even the smallest negative comment or attitude rings so loudly that you might ask yourself, "Did I really used to call this person my friend?"

Negativity will begin to annoy us, but how can we be positive if we are not first tolerant? I am in no way saying that you should stick around negative people, I actually promote the opposite of that, but we should understand that being negative with them is counterproductive.

Because we want to distance ourselves from that negativity, when you speak to these people who are stuck in that vicious cycle, speak to them about the positive things happening.

Spread joy, give them a compliment, and remember that a smile goes a long way in turning someone's negative day into a glimmer of hope for something better.

With wisdom we will learn to carefully remove ourselves from their space. We cannot stay angry at negative people. We owe them the opportunity to learn as we have learned.

Give them this book as gift from your heart. Offer them a way to see the love in the world and the light inside themselves. Have a talk with them. The chances that we can influence negativity with our positivity are far greater than the chances that we will be influenced by negativity.

Becoming a Loner

The more positive you become, the more you want to spend time with yourself. There is a new love for understanding ourselves when we are positive.

We tend to enjoy our own company and thoughts, and why shouldn't we? It could get uncomfortable when family or friends expect that you still have all the free time you used to have, and as such, they would still call you up asking for your time.

This is where we learn balance.

As much as we enjoy our own company, we are to share this love, this incredible journey and this new knowledge with others. They need to see the new us and be inspired.

So please make sure to continue to make time for your friends and family, even as you progress on this path of pure positivity and discovering your inner magic.

Feeling Overwhelmed with Possibilities

Finally, there are a lot of possibilities ahead of us when we decide to embrace positive living.

We see for the first time in a long time that we are not limited. We see that whatever we can think of, we can accomplish.

At this point we want to tell everyone what we know, and we want to do so much to prove our new knowledge to the world around us, but this can be overwhelming.

When you find yourself in this phase, take a deep breath and remember that there is enough time for all you have to do. Get a note pad and write down the new plans that have materialized, and from there you will find that things will fall into place.

Allow yourself to embrace the possibilities, and when you have a new idea or goal, write it down! I write everything down. If you could see the sheer number of journals and day planners and dairies I have collected and filled since I first learnt how to write, you would think it was a mini library.

I encourage you to do the same. Buy a pin board or a magnetic white board and hang it in your office or bedroom. Put your goals, your feelings of gratitude, your dreams and desires on it.

Fill it up and look at it every day. Each time something manifests itself that was on your vision board, take it down and thank the Universe profoundly. This makes room for your next big idea. Use post-it notes to write down your goals or mantras, your daily affirmations too, and post those stick notes all over the place!

Post them on your bathroom mirror, so every morning when you're brushing your teeth, you are also filling you mind with positive thoughts and brining your goals to the forefront of your mind.

The more you ENVISION what you want to achieve, the faster you will achieve it!

Live it, breathe it, imagine it and achieve it!

TAKE BABY STEPS

"Don't try to change everything in your life overnight. You will give up and fail if you try to do too much all at once. Instead, focus on making one small change at a time. Sure enough, through consistency of change, you will have a major transformation."
-Sarah Hall

Congratulations on getting to the last chapter of my book! While it's true that you can't master a new skill overnight, starting with opening and reading this book is a huge step towards mastering your mindset and channeling that inner magic you have inside yourself.

There will be moments when you feel discouraged, when you feel like slipping away from this mindset you're striving for. Those moments of weakness are reality checks to build off of, not break you down! Those moments show up just to make sure that you truly want to remain on the path of positivity. They are testing your mindset, testing your strength. Show them who's boss! Show them you've unleashed your inner magic and you know how to use it!

The journey of a thousand miles begins with one step, and no matter how long it would take to reach your final destination, as long as you keep taking one baby step at a time, you will get there.

You can re-read this book when you're feeling a mental block, and let it give you a jump-start so you can maintain momentum.

Now let's take a look at the steps we have learned throughout this book so that you can have a clear focus on what changes you want to bring into your new life, your new way of thinking, your new mindset and your true inner magic.

"Just take the next step.
You don't have to see the whole staircase, just take the next step."
-Martin Luther King Jr

STEP ONE

∞

ACCEPTANCE

You have to be willing to accept who you are and let go of the past. There are many challenges we have to pass through in order to reach our desired destination. Those challenges make us into the person we want to be, or they can break us. We must be strong, accept what we can change, and have the courage and positive outlook to set to work on making those changes. We must learn to be comfortable in our own skin—in being us.

STEP TWO

KNOWLEDGE

Knowledge is power. We have to know the truth in order to move on joyfully in our lives. No matter who we are, at some point in our lives we have believed an erroneous way of thought, and it is only by unlearning those negative thoughts that we can fix what was broken and move forward in positivity.

STEP THREE

DESIRE

 This is the beginning of all achievement. So, if we are to be positive, we must want it, we must desire it, it must be close to an obsession—but not desperation—and we must work towards it.

When we know what we want (and do what it takes to get it) and we know that our desire is something we deserve, we can move quicker to positivity.

STEP FOUR

ACTIVE THOUGHT

This is where it gets interesting. We are to focus on what we want, as well as on positivity to stay positive. All around us there is always one thing or another attempting to dull our joy. We are to persevere by actively letting our thoughts dominate the external situations. We are to find positivity in every situation and use our minds to hold it there.

STEP FIVE

GRATITUDE

Back on the subject of not letting situations or people dull our shine, we turn to gratitude, which is a feeling rather than an act. Gratitude shifts our energy and helps us to notice the good, and uphold it. What we focus on gets bigger and what we ignore fades away. So, it does help to focus on being grateful—on those little things that make for a more positive existence. That way we build up in our lives more of that positivity and love.

STEP SIX

AFFIRMATIONS

This is the act of repeating a positive message to ourselves. The essence of this act is to influence our subconscious in such a way that being positive becomes second nature. The more we repeat a message, the deeper it sinks, and the deeper it sinks, the more real it becomes.

Like casting a magic spell, our dreams can literally become our realities through the power of manifestation, and through mastery of our mindset.

STEP SEVEN

IMAGINATION

Another way of influencing our minds in the direction of being positive is through our imagination. Affirmations deal with words while imagination deals with making images in our minds and generating the feelings associated with those images, as if they were real. You can practice this by closing your eyes and envisioning yourself accomplishing a goal you have, or completing a project. You can also practice this by creating a dream or vision board, and filling it with the successes and goals you have in your life.

STEP EIGHT

PATIENCE

After the influencing has been done, we need to give it time to work and become physical. The positive atmosphere we have created within will be reflected on the outside in its own due time.

And as the changes begin to occur on the outside, we are given more encouragement as to continue in our thought. Remember, patience is a virtue, and good things come to those who wait for the magic to begin to manifest.

STEP NINE

LETTING GO

This is where we talk about persevering in the path of beautifying our inner world. There is no need to force conditions externally. Letting go teaches us that we are to go with the flow of life and let life unfold before us. If you find yourself caught in a situation that is toxic, making you uncomfortable or dulling your shine, then simply BLESS and RELEASE. BLESS that person or situation that causing the negativity, and RELEASE yourself from it.

Let go and move on with your magical self!

STEP TEN

LIVING IN THE MOMENT

This is about being present. Paying attention to a particular task at a time and not letting ourselves get overwhelmed with various activities. Living in the moment helps us enjoy our time here on earth as well as improve our lifestyles, our enjoyment, and, most of all, our positivity.

STEP ELEVEN

SURROUNDINGS

Our surroundings are always showing us exactly where we are in our development as people. A step further from being present is looking around us and seeing exactly what we are being told from the people and things we see every day, as well as the community, street, or room where we find ourselves.

STEP TWELVE

GIVING

The act of giving is a true blessing. It can change someone's day from bad to good, or it can change someone's life forever. A worthy end to a worthy guide.

Now that you know, give back! Share this knowledge with someone else. Once you give something, you can never lose it. Once you teach something, you can never forget it.

AFTERWORD

So, there it is. The magic you have within yourself has always been there. Maybe you knew it was there all along, and you were just looking for someone to stir it up inside you once more. Or perhaps you never knew just quite what you are capable of. Either way, you're here now, and you're as powerful as ever. An energetic being who is filled with new knowledge. Now go on and begin creating the life you've always dreamed of.

Practice, practice, practice... And you will see it takes only consistency to get it right. We can all improve on our positivity until it becomes second nature. And then our only nature.

And always remember,

Life is for the living.

With Love, Sarah Hall

ACKNOWLEDGMENTS

Thank you to my family for their never-ending support, always answering my calls and listening to me through the highs and lows. Whether I called to check in or cry for 20 minutes straight mid mental breakdown, I always know I can count on you and that means everything to me.

I want to acknowledge my mother, Lisa; my father, William; my brother, Justin; my sister, Kaitlyn and my dear sister, Tamara, who passed away July 21st, 2016. You all know the pain I have been through to get to where I am today, and you've experienced the grief with me first hand when we lost Tamara. I love you all so much, my heart is full.

A special thank you to my long-time friend who helped me edit this book the second time around, after years of me debating releasing a (much needed) revision. Mandi Sommer, your sense of humor cheered up this lengthy process.

I also want to send love and gratitude to my friends and fans. Over the years we have been able to grow close, develop relationships and share our stories in a safe place within our community both online and in person. This has made the journey all the more exciting.

Without your endless support, questions and inspiring expressions of self-discovery as we journeyed together on this new positive path, this book would not exist. Being able to share all this with you has given me more inspiration than you know. I can't wait to hear your success stories and break-throughs as you reach for your goals and grab success by the horns.

ABOUT THE AUTHOR

Sarah Hall is an author and mindset coach who lives in London, UK. She was born and raised in Vancouver, Canada. She has written several books on mindset, and she also writes fiction novels. Sarah's passion is helping others to unlock their true potential through her teachings and coaching program.

Sarah inspires others to unleash the magic within themselves to create the life they've always dreamed of having. Sarah has learned through her own journey of self-discovery that there is a special power to be gained through the daily practice of positivity, love and gratitude.

Creating these 12 steps was a mission that Sarah undertook while she was going through the loss of her older sister to a tragic death, on top of trauma and abusive relationships that Sarah decided to grow and evolve from instead of living in a victim mentality.

She created these 12 steps, alongside her coaching program, to help others learn the building blocks that they can use to heal from trauma, grief and pain in order to create a life of abundance, success and joy.

If you're interested in working with Sarah, she takes clients in her coaching programs and has had incredible success helping others to heal their past and build a positive, prosperous future. Visit her website, www.wealthyoptimist.com to learn more.

Follow Sarah Hall

Facebook: Sarah Hall – Wealthy Optimist

http://www.facebook.com/wealthyoptimist

Twitter: SarahHallAuthor

http://www.twitter.com/sarahhallauthor

Instagram: SarahHallAuthor

http://www.instagram.com/sarahhallauthor

LinkedIn: SarahHallAuthor

http://linkedin.com/in/sarahhallauthor

YouTube: Wealthy Optimist

http://www.youtube.com/c/wealthyoptimist

Wealthy Optimist Mindset Facebook Community Group:

https://www.facebook.com/groups/wealthyoptimistmindset

Blog: Wealthy Optimist

http://www.wealthyoptimist.com

Podcast: Wealthy Optimist

https://podcasts.apple.com/gb/podcast/wealthy-optimist-podcast/id1514471062

ALSO BY THE AUTHOR

Rao Unveiled

Printed in Great Britain
by Amazon